Gentle light by night

Made in Sweden

Born in 1949. Thousands of new configurations yet to be discovered.

Movie set designer Miriam Myrtell's configuration. Discovered in 2021.
stringfurniture.com/miriammyrtell

string®

KINFOLK

MAGAZINE	**EDITOR-IN-CHIEF**	John Clifford Burns
	EDITOR	Harriet Fitch Little
	ART DIRECTOR	Christian Møller Andersen
	DESIGN DIRECTOR	Alex Hunting
	COPY EDITOR	Rachel Holzman
	FACT CHECKER	Gabriele Dellisanti
	DESIGN INTERN	Bethany Rush

STUDIO	**ADVERTISING DIRECTOR**	Edward Mannering
	SALES & DISTRIBUTION DIRECTOR	Edward Mannering
	STUDIO & PROJECT MANAGER	Susanne Buch Petersen
	DESIGNER & ART DIRECTOR	Staffan Sundström
	DIGITAL MANAGER	Cecilie Jegsen

STYLING, HAIR & MAKEUP

Afaf Ali, Malin Åsard Wallin, Dominick Barcelona, Taan Doan, Andreas Frienholt, Helena Henrion, Seongseok Oh, Nadia Pizzimenti, David de Quevedo, Ian Russell, Gabe Shin, Zalya Shokarova, Seunghee Son, Sasha Stroganova, Camille-Joséphine Teisseire, Ronnie Tremblay

WORDS

Allyssia Alleyne, Alex Anderson, Rima Sabina Aouf, Katie Calautti, Stephanie d'Arc Taylor, Cody Delistraty, Gabriele Dellisanti, Daphnée Denis, Tom Faber, Bella Gladman, Nikolaj Hansson, Harry Harris, Nathan Ma, Stevie Mackenzie-Smith, Kyla Marshell, Micah Nathan, Megan Nolan, Okechukwu Nzelu, Stephanie Phillips, Debika Ray, Asher Ross, Rhian Sasseen, Charles Shafaieh, Pip Usher, Salome Wagaine, Annick Weber

ARTWORK & PHOTOGRAPHY

Sara Abraham, Gustav Almestål, Ted Belton, Katrien de Blauwer, Luc Braquet, Niccolò Caranti, Valerie Chiang, Giseok Cho, Adrien Dirand, Lasse Fløde, Bea de Giacomo, Oberto Gili, Mac Gramlich, Josh Hight, Victoria Ivanova, Cecilie Jegsen, Douglas Kirkland, Brigitte Lacombe, Romain Laprade, Fanny Latour-Lambert, Nina Leen, Frank Leonardo, Anastasia Lisitsyna, Salva López, Andrew Meredith, Christian Møller Andersen, Inge Morath, Gordon Parks, Piczo, Marcus Schäfer, Yana Sheptovetskaya, Lulu Sylbert, Armin Tehrani, Emma Trim, Leonardo Anker Amadeus Vanda, Andre D. Wagner, Weekend Creative, Paloma Wool, Corey Woosley, Maggie Zhu

CROSSWORD	Anna Gundlach
PUBLICATION DESIGN	Alex Hunting Studio
COVER PHOTOGRAPH	Ted Belton

Kinfolk (ISSN 2596-6154) is published quarterly by Ouur ApS, Amagertorv 14, 1, 1160 Copenhagen, Denmark. Printed by Park Communications Ltd in London, United Kingdom. Color reproduction by Park Communications Ltd in London, United Kingdom. All rights reserved. No part of this publication may be reproduced, distributed or transmitted in any form or by any means, including photocopying or other electronic or mechanical methods, without prior written permission of the editor in chief, except in the case of brief quotations embodied in critical reviews and certain other noncommercial uses permitted by copyright law. The US annual subscription price is $87 USD. Airfreight and mailing in the USA by WN Shipping USA, 156-15, 146th Avenue, 2nd Floor, Jamaica, NY 11434, USA. Application to mail at periodicals postage prices is pending at Jamaica NY 11431. US Postmaster: Send address changes to Kinfolk, WN Shipping USA, 156-15, 146th Avenue, 2nd Floor, Jamaica, NY 11434, USA. Subscription records are maintained at Ouur ApS, Amagertorv 14, 1, 1160 Copenhagen, Denmark. The views expressed in Kinfolk magazine are those of the respective contributors and are not necessarily shared by the company or its staff. SUBSCRIBE: Kinfolk is published four times a year. To subscribe, visit www.kinfolk.com/subscribe or email us at info@kinfolk.com. CONTACT US: If you have questions or comments, please write to us at info@kinfolk.com. For advertising and partnership inquiries, get in touch at advertising@kinfolk.com.

HOUSE OF
FINN JUHL

Finn Juhl | 45 Chair | 1945

finnjuhl.com

Starters

12 – 44

Features

46 – 112

"With each space, I want to tell a new story."
PIERRE YOVANOVITCH — P. 55

CONTENTS

Photograph: Romain Laprade

Youth

Directory

114 – 176

178 – 192

"I want young people to choose compassion."
NIC STONE — P. 153

Photograph: Romain Laprade

nature, delivered.

Genovese basil

Individually formative and culturally formidable, youth looms large in the collective imagination. For those who can no longer be considered young, it is often rose-tinted with the memory of rebellion, irresponsibility and the short-lived belief that infinite futures lie just over the horizon. For those who are young today, the reality is a bit more complicated.

Elise By Olsen, the 21-year-old editor-in-chief of fashion magazine *Wallet*, interviewed on page 114, has been working since the age of 13 to get the fashion industry to actually listen to the young people it fetishizes. Although she no longer believes that she—or anyone—should try to speak on behalf of a generation, she still uses her unusual power to hold the fashion business to account. For *Wallet*'s inaugural issue, she asked her industry elders a deceptively simple question: *Who gains from your influence or power... except you?*

Throughout Issue Thirty-Nine, we've tried to balance the open-faced optimism of youth with the sobering realities of growing up at a time when it can feel like the world is closing in rather than unfurling before you. Nic Stone, the bestselling young adult fiction author interviewed on page 146, puts it best: "I want my readers to know what's out there, but I also want them to know that they get to decide how they are going to move to the world and what they believe about themselves," she says. In Note to Self on page 154, we offer a glimpse into the complicated formative years of some of our favorite people; six past interviewees have written letters to their teenage selves. And in Awkward, our fashion editorial on page 138, we celebrate the humor of the scenarios that we failed to see the funny side of the first time around, such as turning up at a party in the same outfit as your friend.

Also in the issue, we take a tour of designer Pierre Yovanovitch's meticulously restored Provencal château, drink wine with sommelier Grace Mahary and meet the queen of internet comedy Eva Victor. Over short columns and long essays, our writers examine the big questions of the season: Why is late-night TV no longer funny? Is it ever okay to make your child an Instagram influencer? And why on earth does every milk carton now read like it was written by a second-rate stand-up comedian?

JOHN CLIFFORD BURNS & HARRIET FITCH LITTLE

Premium Subscription

Become a Premium Subscriber for $75 per year, and you'll receive four
print issues of the magazine and full access to our online archives, plus a
set of *Kinfolk* notecards and a wide range of special offers.

1.

Starters

12—44

Half a Notion

A reassessment of ambivalence.

Words change meaning over time, and the way it happens can reveal secrets about the culture that's changing them. Take ambivalence. For many of us, it has come to refer to an absence of opinion: "You choose, I don't care." Traditionally, however, it refers to the simultaneous presence of contradictory feelings and attitudes. It's a surprisingly young word, coined by Swiss psychiatrist Eugen Bleuler in 1910. Soon after, it was adopted by Freud, who saw that ambivalence—particularly the coexistence of love and hatred toward the same person—was a fundamental aspect of human experience. You don't need to read Freud to understand his thrust, you just need a sibling.

Melanie Klein, the great psychoanalyst and observer of children, had a more touching take on Freud's theories. She taught that infants don't yet conceive of parents as individual human beings. There is merely the "good" mother who scoops us up, and the "bad" mother who puts us down. As we grow, it dawns on us that both these figures are parts of the same person, and our long, disappointing journey with ambivalence begins. [1]

Many of us are *afraid* of our own ambivalence. And why wouldn't we be? It asks us to admit to feelings and desires that might face cruel rejection by those we admire. To be awake to our own contradictions may make life richer, but it's hard work. Some of the most transcendent pleasures in life seem to promise a reprieve from that struggle. When we fall deeply in love, we see no wrong in our lover. Without knowing it, we worship them for restoring what we thought had been lost forever. Inevitably, though, our own ambivalence resurfaces. We remember that we have our own mind, and worse yet, our lover does too.

But a part of us never stops hoping, and that hope can be manipulated to terrible ends. As long as there have been politics, there have been politicians promising a return to the good old days, when right and wrong were clear and simple. We're susceptible to this myth not because we believe it is historically accurate, but because we ourselves did experience such a time, in a way, before we ever learned to speak. [2]

Online, ambivalence is all but forbidden. We feel pressured to deny it in ourselves, and to attack it in others. To declare what side we're on. After all, with so much deep injustice, who has time for contradictions? The relief we feel among our closest friends is a refuge from this; they take what we say in the context of who we are, their love for us, and their trust in our conscience. And as a reward they get our uncensored intimacy and laughter.

My own psychoanalyst once once said that "denial of our own ambivalence is the road to tyranny of the self, and intolerance of ambivalence in others is the road to totalitarianism." These roads have historically been open to people of all temperaments, on the right and the left. We avoid them by listening to ourselves—our real selves—and distinguishing thought from action. We must acknowledge and confront our rage toward the innocent, our attraction to the dastardly. Like the plots of dreams, these feelings are almost never what they first seem.

Indifference in the face of injustice is wrong. We must decide what we think is right in life, and act on it. But to be ambivalent in even the deepest matters is human. It would be a good world that remembered the difference.

Words by Asher Ross

NOTES

1. Ambivalence has become a useful framework for evaluating sexism. In the late 1990s, researchers Peter Glick and Susan Fiske pioneered the Ambivalent Sexism Inventory: a more nuanced model for understanding sexism, which accounted for positive as well as negative stereotypes held about women.

2. Political ambivalence, understood correctly, isn't apathy. An ambivalent voter would be one who held two contradictory notions to be true: for example, a strong belief in individual liberty combined with a desire for the state to sanction certain behaviors.
—

Photograph: *Time* by Leonardo Anker Amadeus Vandal, 2018

Featuring 41 hand-designed patterns, Du Pasquier's collection of tiles for Mutina presents an almost overwhelming range of possible permutations.

Photography: Bea de Giacomo

At the age of 22, French artist Nathalie Du Pasquier moved from her hometown of Bordeaux to Milan where she joined designer Ettore Sottsass in founding the Memphis Group, an influential collective of young artists who expressed their opposition to modernist trends through an oeuvre of brightly colored, oddly shaped designs. After over three decades of exclusively dedicating herself to painting, she discusses her recent collaboration with Italian ceramics brand Mutina on Mattonelle Margherita—her first-ever tile collection—and the role of color in her creations. *Interview by Gabriele Dellisanti*

GD: *Your work has always been characterized by its use of vibrant color combinations. Why do they appeal to you?* **NDP:** Colors might be prevalent in my work but they only become vibrant when they are placed next to certain other colors. For example, Mattonelle Margherita is characterized by a wide range of different colors, but you can choose between creating a simple layout or a bold, vibrant one.

GD: *You crafted the Mattonelle Margherita collection for Mutina. How did you find the right balance between keeping the design minimal while fully expressing your creativity?* **NDP:** I think there is nothing minimal in the design of Mattonelle Margherita. I wasn't interested in just expressing my creativity, but in finding interesting ways of playing with simple signs and colors. I drew the patterns by hand and developed a new range of paintings for the project.

GD: *How do patterns make use of color and allow for multiple layouts?*

NDP: I didn't want to create preestablished layouts and combinations; I wanted to give the user the freedom to design their own. The collection allows for many possibilities: The elements can be used to cover entire floors and walls or to create decorative details within any home. It's really all about your own creativity.

GD: *In your art, you often create 3D compositions that you then paint. What's the appeal of working this way, rather than painting scenes from real life?* **NDP:** The appeal of representing abstract objects is in avoiding the narration of a story. If I paint things from the studio or from the kitchen, like I've done many times, there is always a story attached to them and the viewer will probably see symbols or other ideas, something I am not too interested in. Still, I paint these abstract constructions from real life and they are totally figurative.

GD: *Did you also paint the brick monuments you made for Mutina's BRIC exhibition last year?* **NDP:** Actually, I never paint big things. I'd rather say that I paint small things big, and those monuments are definitely not small! The bricks in the exhibition were chosen from a catalog and painted by a master craftsman, then I gave precise instructions to build the structures that formed the exhibition.

GD: *What does a brightly tiled surface bring to a space that paint can't achieve?* **NDP:** The housewife in me says: A tiled surface is easy to clean and always looks new!

—

This feature was produced in partnership with Mutina.

What the Duck

An introduction to duck architecture.

For 40 years, photographer and historian John Margolies drove across America photographing roadside architecture. He documented coffee shops shaped like coffeepots, hot dog-shaped fast-food stands, even a Shell gas station that looked like, you guessed it, a giant scallop shell. Margolies had appreciated these unpretentious buildings since he was a kid, and he captured them unsentimentally.

These joyfully literal buildings have a name: architectural ducks. The term—coined by Denise Scott Brown, Robert Venturi and Steven Izenour in their seminal book, *Learning from Las Vegas*—describes structures that incorporate their function into their very fabric. The concrete Big Duck shop, built by a Long Island duck farmer, inspired the moniker. Scott Brown, Venturi and Izenour differentiated architectural ducks from the more commonplace "decorated sheds"—functional buildings with ornamental signage. In the post-World War II years, ducks were ubiquitous along American roadsides. Car culture was booming, and the new interstate highway system created an imperative for businesses to quickly communicate their purpose.

While these buildings were adored by bored kids in backseats, and seen as vernacular totems by locals, they've historically been polarizing—and not just because they skew toward kitsch. Scott Brown, Venturi and Izenour argued that a duck's function and structure are subservient to the symbol of the building. "From a modernist standpoint, that's not necessarily seen as the correct way of approaching design," explains Luke Pearson, a lecturer at London's Bartlett School of Architecture. But Pearson believes that there's pleasure in their literalness: "It detaches us from the idea of pure efficiency." Instead, when an ice-cream shop is shaped like an ice-cream cone, "the building becomes tied to a very particular history encapsulated in its architectural form."

Most of the roadside landmarks Margolies documented are no longer standing; they were torn down to make way for uniform chain stores or they simply fell into disrepair. But there's refreshing optimism in a witty architectural interjection designed to make you look, think, and maybe even laugh. Architecture critic Paul Goldberger described ducks as "exclamation points of the landscape," and what's not to love about that?
Words by Stevie Mackenzie-Smith

MORE PRODUCT
by Pip Usher

Once upon a time, a product was simply an item offered for sale. But this capitalistic shorthand has undergone a makeover that now sees it glowing with an aspirational sheen. Used as industry jargon for any manner of cosmetics or haircare, "product" has transformed the vagueness of its meaning into an attribute. On Netflix's makeover show *The Home Edit*, "go get product" (meaning, in this case, filing cabinets and boxes) is the catch-all solution to organizational woes. Much like a mysterious guest at a party, the word gives nothing away—and because of this ambiguity, it suddenly becomes covetable. Not convinced? Try describing your "hair product" or shampoo as "a viscous liquid used to clean wet hair." No matter how fancy the brand, it'll instantly lose its allure.

Left Photograph: Yana Sheptovetskaya for *British Vogue*. Right Photograph: Weekend Creative

On Wackaging

Your milk carton is not your friend.

Back in 2014, *The Guardian* asked: "Why on earth is food describing itself in the first person?" Now *Kinfolk* asks it again. The chatty tone, the casual ad copy—the printed equivalent of a server who sits in your booth and writes their name on your placemat—is ostensibly a rejection of corporate stoicism and a return to those mythical times when companies cared about their customers. Personification used to be the purview of poets; now it's mandatory for lettuce to remind you that it prefers to be kept in the crisper. Coca-Cola insists it is here to "refresh the world and make a difference," which is eye-rolling but at least open in its ambition for global dominance; contrast this with Chipotle's bag-copy ("Don't be a jerk. Try to love everyone,") or Oatly's directions for their Barista Edition oat drink: "Warm it, foam it and drink it straight. Trust me."

Who is the "me"? The company? The copywriter? The drink itself? Is the imperative "Trust me" supposed to be earnest? Postmodern? Why should anyone preemptively trust an oat milk? How does Chipotle define "jerk"? What, exactly, does trying to "love everyone" have to do with burritos? Should an order of chips and guac come with platitudes?

The argument may be that infiltrating a customer's moral code with a kind of secular theism, a meaningful message hidden in jaunty tones, creates the deepest kind of brand loyalty. And because customers are now savvy to the machinations of advertising—mostly due to the advertisers themselves—there's no good reason for companies to maintain the artifice. Yes, we want to sell you something; Yes, you know we want to sell you something; Yes, we know you know. So how about we all stop playing games and have a real chat?

Of course there's nothing real about it. The chat is still a sales pitch—more than that, it's a focused seduction posing as a no-agenda conversation. At least corporate stoicism respected its customers enough to not pretend the customers saw their relationship as anything more than transactional. This newish strategy is a repackaged lie. Gone is the suit, the humorless adman, the instructions and ingredients written in bland, technical terms; now the robot wears human skin. Join us. We love you.

Words by Micah Nathan

CALM AND COLLECTED
by Pip Usher

When Francesco Clemente moved to New York City in 1981, the Italian painter fell in with the city's experimental art scene. Clemente—who produces vivid, pastel-hued paintings of the human form—was already being heralded as a leader of the "return to figuration" movement; his new friends included visionary street artist Jean-Michel Basquiat and Pop Art icon Andy Warhol.

The three men decided to embark on a creative collaboration. Each would start a painting and leave enough space for the other two to contribute their ideas to the canvas. It wasn't the first time that Clemente had partnered with others. After first visiting India in the '70s, he'd become fascinated by craftsmanship, and used the talents of artisans from Jaipur and Orissa for *Francesco Clemente Pinxit*, a series of miniatures that he produced. Around the same time that he joined forces with Basquiat and Warhol, Clemente was also producing works to accompany the words of Beat poet Allen Ginsberg.

In Clemente's Greenwich Village townhouse, an eclectic collection of art has accumulated over the years. In the living room, a towering wooden sculpture from the South Pacific stands beside Henry Fuseli's 18th-century painting *Head of Satan*. They're an unexpected pairing—and yet, as Clemente's own career can testify, sometimes that's what works best. *Photograph by Oberto Gili*

New Challenge

THE IKEA EFFECT
by Pip Usher

If you find yourself irritated and confused halfway through putting together an item of flat-packed furniture, take comfort: It's likely you'll end up appreciating it more than if you'd bought it assembled. This psychological phenomenon—dubbed the IKEA Effect—refers to a cognitive bias whereby consumers overvalue products that require a degree of labor from them. For brands, this is wonderful news. By asking consumers to do some of the legwork, they can inflate its sentimental value. Make the assemblage too tricky, though, and the ploy could backfire. As the academics responsible for the term explain, "labor leads to love only when that labor is successful." (Top: Stoja table lamp. Center: Stoja pendant lamp. Bottom: Vilbert chair. All products are vintage IKEA.)

Will TikTok change choreography?

Anywhere you go in the world, you can find the same café. You know the aesthetic: hanging plants, exposed brick, raw concrete. This ubiquitous aesthetic is traceable to Instagram. As the platform grew, businesses that wanted to attract the young and hip began taking design cues from the most popular Instagram photos. Interiors began to be designed *from* Instagram *for* Instagram.

The social media platform made millennial-chic interior design accessible to the aesthetically inclined from Tokyo to Tulsa. But Instagram, if you ask a Gen Zer, is desperately unhip. The social media platform *du jour* is TikTok, and the things people post most frequently on TikTok are snippets of themselves dancing. Could TikTok have the same impact on choreography as Instagram did on interior design?

You can find gymnasts, cheerleaders, and professional dancers of all stripes on TikTok. These tastemakers post micro-videos of themselves performing choreography ranging from a G-rated two-step to something that should come with a warning label. The catchiest dances then seep out through various TikTok communities until they saturate youth culture as a whole.

From there, the amateurs take over. The most successful TikTok dance videos are the ones where the dancer is clearly having a ball. What's more, the medium revels in iteration. Professionals post half-speed videos of themselves doing difficult dances for people who want to learn, as well as tutorials breaking down the hardest moves. The dances change as they filter through the platform, as each new dancer adds their own flourish. Not every attempt is a success: In August, one TikTok user was hospitalized after attempting the so-called "WAP" dance, inspired by Cardi B and Megan Thee Stallion's summer banger

Part of the appeal of the Instagram aesthetic is that those white backgrounds and dusky purple succulents look good when seen on a phone. Similarly, the most popular TikTok dances (see "Renegade" and "Say So") are designed to be viewed in a vertical camera frame. Hence, they consist primarily of arm movements easy enough to be performed while standing—or even sitting—relatively still. They might be bringing choreography to the masses, but Alvin Ailey these kids decidedly are not.

Dancing well isn't their end goal, however. Rather, they're using dance as a conduit to fun. And in doing so, they may make choreographed dance more accessible. If Laura Dern is getting in on the action, it's only a matter of time before Aunt Margaret is doing the "Toosie Slide" at Sunday lunch.
Words by Stephanie d'Arc Taylor

Left Photographs: Courtesy of The IKEA Museum. Right Photograph: Anastasia Lisitsyna for MY812

Photograph: Paloma Wool

Flash Back

On the decline of the flash mob fad.

The concept is radical in its simplicity. An email or text is circulated among friends, friends of friends, or strangers. Participants flock to a designated public place, where they spontaneously engage in something out of the ordinary and, in doing so, astound onlookers: A Michael Jackson dance tribute, a lightsaber battle, a pillow fight. It's systematized, attention-grabbing, and over in minutes.

In the decade following the first Manhattan flash mobs in 2003, these random acts of weirdness seemed a fun way to engage with the internet and mobile technology at a point when their value and purpose were still largely undefined.

What a difference 20 years makes. In the age of social media, we accept as a given that virtual communication can lead to all manner of real-world action. Tyler, the Creator can announce a surprise show on Twitter and Instagram, and summon hundreds of fans to a London venue in the middle of the afternoon, while demonstrators in Hong Kong regularly appropriate flash-mob tactics to thwart the police and avoid prosecution.

So why does the flash-mob concept feel so dated? Perhaps the biggest change is that the internet is no longer seen as merely a digital gateway to physical interactions; it's a universe unto itself. We build networks of LinkedIn contacts and Twitter followers we have no intention of ever meeting, and even our IRL friendships must be remotely nurtured in WhatsApp chats, Instagram Stories and FaceTime calls. In this climate, the flash mob is about as innovative as the 1950s fad for stuffing as many people as possible into a phone box.

That's not to say the flash mob has died out entirely. Every now and then, a flash-mob-style marriage proposal or musical performance finds its way into our news feeds. But it's not the same—not really. Even these real-world actions are now planned with online virality in mind.

More than anything, the flash mob stands as a relic of a certain Web 1.0 attitude toward the internet: a naivete, optimism and excitement that can only exist at the start of something new. While those early flash mobs may live on in image archives and YouTube clips, that enthusiastic spirit is much harder to recapture.

Words by Allyssia Alleyne

rell

...or a not-so-new concept, *umarell* refers to an ... his days inspecting the work in progress at ... word was coined in 2005 by Danilo Masotti, ... a distortion of *umarèl*, meaning "old man" in Bolo... ...ce it describes what is traditionally a group phenomenon, it... ...tant to know that the correct plural is the Anglicized form *umarells*, not the standard Italian plural *umarelli*. This is to help simplify the use of the word in languages other than Italian.

Meaning: You see them from about 8 a.m. on town squares, sidewalks or street corners, peeking through construction site fencing to catch a glimpse of what's happening on the other side. By 10 a.m., a small crowd has usually gathered for live commentary. They aren't hard hat-wearing engineers, however, but umarells: retired men in flat caps and beige coats, standing with their hands clasped behind their backs, watching the workers.

As much as the word is patronizing, even mocking, the concept has given rise to a number of well-meaning community initiatives that celebrate an overlooked demographic. In the Bologna region, where the term originated, various towns have launched rewards for their vigilant elderly residents, from paying small stipends for overseeing unattended worksites to awarding "umarell of the year" badges to the most diligent public servants. In 2016, the phenomenon even caught the attention of US chain Burger King, which initiated an Italy-wide social media campaign to recruit umarells for their newly planned sites in the hope of winning over the hearts of the famously fast-food-loathing nation.

Although the word hasn't yet made it into the Oxford English Dictionary, the Urban Dictionary entry helps put it in a wider context. According to its definition, umarells aren't just lingering around Italian construction sites, they are everywhere; they are "people in a community who offer all sorts of comments to those who are trying to get some work done, but who are not doing any work themselves." Whether it's a colleague, a supervisor or a neighbor, everyone knows an umarell—and, perhaps, everyone also needs an umarell. Aren't we all more productive if we have someone peeking over our shoulder to check if we're actually getting things done?

Words by Annick Weber

In 2017, Italian manufacturers Superstuff had a surprise hit with its 3D-printed desktop figurine of an umarell. The 6-inch-tall man, designed to motivate distraction-prone office workers, became one of the country's most popular holiday gifts.

Erika de Casier

In conversation with a romantic soul.

Erika de Casier began making music right after her high school years. A decade on, the Copenhagen-based musician has fashioned a path from sweet, self-produced R&B to remixing Dua Lipa, releasing her 2019 album *Essentials* and signing with renowned independent record label 4AD. Along the way, she's learned to produce songs from scratch, with the help of an occasional YouTube tutorial. "I can make music anywhere, so long as I have my computer and a pair of headphones," says de Casier. She creates music that trills with different emotions—those of the heart, and those that come with the nerve-racking transition from making bedroom beats to performing to large crowds. As she sings in one 2020 release, her first with 4AD: "No butterflies, no nothing." *Interview by Nikolaj Hansson.*

NH: *You've lived in Portugal, the US and now Denmark, with parents from Belgium and Cape Verde. How do you think this geographic pluralism has shaped your music?* **EDC:** You're making it sound more globe-trotting than it actually is! I was raised in Portugal until the age of eight, when we moved to Denmark where I've lived ever since, bar one year of high school in the US. I didn't grow up with my dad, but my mom was the one who encouraged me to explore the arts. She worked a lot during my upbringing, meaning that my brother and I spent a lot of time on our own, doing whatever we wanted to—watching movies, playing games, eating pizza. It was very free in a way. I was drawing and painting for hours and hours and I think that this ability to fully immerse myself into a particular process is something that I often employ when creating music today.

Photography: Armin Tehrani / Værnis Studio

> *"There are so many songs that I've made that I'll never play for a living soul, and that make me appreciate the invention of headphones."*

NH: *Back then, did you want to become a musician?* **EDC:** No. I don't remember ever having that singular thought of, "Oh, I want to become a musician." I didn't have a musical upbringing or any real interest in making music until a much later point in life. The dream of becoming a pop star—the type that stood on stage with a headset microphone on their head—was there when I was a kid and so was the act of singing in front of the mirror with a hairbrush as a prop microphone but there wasn't more to it than that. I accidentally signed up for music class instead of Spanish in high school and was too ashamed to admit it, so on the first day there I just went along with it. Maybe I was a bit intrigued as well. I wasn't a great singer and couldn't read notes either, but I really liked singing, so I kept on going. I had an unbelievable amount of stage fright but again kept on moving forward and the same can be said for producing music on my own; I was really bad at it, but found myself having fun, so I kept at it.

NH: *You still produce some of your own songs. How do you find that these differ from the ones that are produced by other people?* **EDC:** I think that they differ in the sense that music is always the result of the composer's mind—whichever references, tastes, experiences, beliefs, skills, moods and ways of working that they find themselves gravitating toward in that particular moment. If there are more heads in the game when making a song, the actual sound that comes out will be a reflection of that. It's important to feel that the people working with you are an asset to the music. I'm very particular about what I want to make and who I want to work with. I've sometimes pondered whether that makes me a snob, but I think that one should choose musical partners with the same level of consideration as one does romantic partners, because both things are equally gratifyingly joyful as well as intense. One of the people that I work with the closest is Natal Zaks. He's an old friend and this shines through in our process. It's basically me coming up with a sketch—a beat with some lyrics and a form—and then we go from there.

NH: *How does intuition play into your way of making music?* **EDC:** It plays a big role; you play something, then a part of it catches your ear, then you follow that to wherever it takes you. You might like it or maybe you won't, then you head somewhere else and see where that goes.

Trusting your intuition is a crucial element to making music so long as it doesn't shelter you off from the influences and ideas of others. I only have one rule when making music: You can never say no. When you show to yourself and others that all ideas are worth a shot, that intangible feeling of creative freedom flourishes in the room and it's from that feeling that truly great ideas can emerge.

NH: *Making music is about intuition, but it's also about technical ability. How do you balance those two things?* **EDC:** To me, they go hand in hand when producing—my technical skills are a vehicle for creative expression, which probably can be said for any instrument, really. The more time you spend doing a certain thing, the more natural it will feel and the freer you will be in a creative sense. I'm still learning with every song that I make; sometimes I have to watch a tutorial on YouTube on a certain thing to be able to get to where I want to go. It's not quite as romantic as a jamming session but it is a necessity in order for me to progress.

NH: *Putting the technical aspect aside and zoning in on the ethos of making music, do you find that, more than anything else, it is about cultivating an emotional release?* **EDC:** Partially, yes. Most of us have so much noise rumbling around inside of our heads—worries about the future or thoughts of the past, things we should've said or things that were said by others. We're forever analyzing the behaviors of ourselves and others. Music can just as much be an escape from all of that as it can be self-indulgent. If you're lucky, you'll find yourself recognizing parts of you in someone else's music and that can be a beautiful thing, though sometimes it can get too close—when it reminds you of something that you'd rather forget, like smelling the scent of a person that you miss. It switches on your senses in an emotional way and what's most interesting about this is that it's an individual thing—we might find ourselves connecting deeply with a song that the person next to us will find to be trash. This is what makes releasing your own music such a truly nerve-racking experience because most of us are unable to separate the maker from the person. There are so many songs that I've made that I'll never play for a living soul, and that make me appreciate the invention of headphones. Music is a personal thing.

De Casier attributes her '90s-inspired sound to her childhood: When she first moved to Denmark in 1998, she couldn't speak Danish, so she spent her free time watching MTV.

Location: The Audo, Copenhagen

Liana Finck

The wobbly-lined cartoonist with a razor-sharp vision.

Cartoonist Liana Finck loves art that makes you feel seen, or explains something that you've needed explaining. It's exactly how her half a million Instagram followers might describe her own cartoons, which are by turns funny, angry or thoughtful, rendered in just a few jittery lines of black ink. Her work regularly appears in *The New Yorker*, and she has also authored the graphic novels *Passing for Human* and *A Bintel Brief* and the cartoon collection *Excuse Me*. When we speak, she is at home in Park Slope, Brooklyn, working on her new book *Let There Be Light*, a take on the Book of Genesis with a female God. *Interview by Rima Sabina Aouf*

RSA: *You draw with a distinctive, wavering line. What role does imperfection play in your work?* **LF:** My natural line is sloppy, but I always tried to draw neat. I remember worshipping Saul Steinberg, the cartoonist, when I was younger. He has this suave line with a slight vibrato in it, like a little wiggle—a wiggle that you wouldn't have unless you had perfect control. My mom draws the same way. She, like Steinberg, trained as an architect, and I think it's like an old-school architect's line maybe. But I think both Instagram and also getting a little bit of professional success—and feeling like someone wanted my work, so I couldn't redo it a million times—helped me get past the perfectionism. And I think I do have a confident line now. It's the confidence that matters. A sloppy line that's not confident is not great. And you get confidence by having some measure of entitlement.

    RSA: *What do you like about having Instagram as your main publishing platform?* **LF:** Social media gave me a chance to just put my real self out there instead of trying to cater to the people who were the gatekeepers. It made me able to make work that felt real rather than phony. I would have arrived at that at some point, but maybe more like at age 60. And instead I feel like I got there at age 28, and that's great.

    RSA: *I love your advice column for* The New Yorker, Dear Pepper. *How did you come to do it from the point of view of a dog?* **LF:** The roundabout reason is I was trying to figure out the name for an advice column, and I wanted to reference Dear Sugar. I came up with Dear Pepper, and Pepper was my childhood dog. But also, I relate to dogs. For whatever reason, I feel like I don't really know how humans act in any given situation. It just doesn't come naturally to me. I'm always watching, and I wanted to translate that into an advice column. Like, this dog is very aware of how humans act because she's had to study it.

    RSA: *The last year has been challenging for everyone. What have been some of the highs and lows for you?* **LF:** Seeing people suffering has been hard, but also the paranoia is wearying. When the pandemic was at its peak, my boyfriend and I were washing our clothes in the bathtub every time we went outside. It was a lot. But the highs have been really high. I've enjoyed not having a lot of plans and not taking the subway and not seeing people—or not *not* seeing people, but seeing people close to home and in less hectic situations. I'm realizing how much I like my friends. And my boyfriend moved in before he'd been planning to because we were quarantining together, and I really like living with him. I feel like we've become adults very fast. We were like freewheeling people, going to bars and museums and parties a lot, and now we're getting a dog and cooking a lot. I used to be so afraid of this happening. But I like it. It's good.

Photograph: Josh Hight Photography for Begg & Co

State of Mind

A short history of micronations.

In the 1960s, when Roy Bates set up a radio station on an abandoned ex-naval fort in the middle of the North Sea, he was not looking to build a nation. Bates, once a major in the British Army, was only trying to circumvent broadcasting laws. The British government did not take kindly to his pirate station, and Bates was forced to retreat.[1] So it was that, in 1967, he took to another abandoned fortress, this time outside UK jurisdiction, and established Sealand. With his wife and children, Bates declared the tower a principality. It became a micronation—an entity that claims to be a sovereign state but is not internationally recognized. Describing itself as the world's smallest country, Sealand covers all of 0.004 square miles. In lieu of taxes, it sells memorabilia, from personalized coats of arms ($219.99) to duchies, which confer membership of the Sealand nobility ($656.53).

Bates, though isolated, is not unique. In 1970, Australian citizen Leonard Casley founded The Principality of Hutt River after an agricultural dispute with the government. He declared himself a prince, and his 29 square miles a principality. And in 2018, Guernsey resident Steve Ogier responded to a planning permission refusal by declaring his land an independent country. He became a king overnight.

The act of founding a nation may seem foreign, but the motivation behind it is not. Most of us have secretly wondered if life would be easier if we had more control over that pesky red tape, those uneven road surfaces, that meddling political leader. The seductive idea that it is other people who mess things up for us (rather than life itself being messy) knows no borders.

Thus the fascination with micronations is real and widespread. Freetown Christiania, a partially autonomous commune in Copenhagen, for example, has hosted large numbers of tourists, and gentrification has recently forced some long-term residents to leave.[2] People visit, wanting to admire what the founders have done, or to chuckle at the shortcomings of a dream made more-or-less real. Perhaps, though, tourists are also drawn by the chance to take a look at the road not taken: Who among us hasn't imagined another life where we get to make our own rules?

Unlike breakaway states, which pose real political danger, micronations are generally treated as benign oddities by the international community. The Australian government appeared to turn a blind eye while Hutt River State printed its own passports and driving licenses. Sadly, though, some realities of citizenship are harder to avoid. When Prince Casley died in 2019, his son was left with a $2.15 million tax bill, forcing him to sell the land to pay the debt. After 50 years, the principality returned whence it came: an idea.

Other micronations survive, however. The UK government meant to destroy all its abandoned ex-naval forts, and yet Sealand (once known as Fort Roughs) remains. A tiny outpost, ruled (like most micronations) by one man, it is quietly allowed to exist. Its motto? "E Mare, Libertas": "From the sea, freedom."

Words by Okechukwu Nzelu

NOTES

1. Despite Bates' battles with the government, he didn't feel any solidarity with fellow legal mavericks. He forcibly evicted the operators of another pirate radio station to claim the abandoned platform. One radio operator was shot through the ear and another lost a finger during the struggle.

2. A lack of affordable housing in Copenhagen was one of the main reasons why squatters occupied Christiania and declared it a freetown in 1971. Fifty years later, the push to "normalize" Christiania under Danish tax law has made rental costs prohibitive for some long-time residents.

Much of the wine we drink comes from grapes grown in vast vineyards across the Mediterranean, Australia and California. But a small movement of urban growers is proving that an inner-city parcel of land can make not only a worthy vineyard, but a defiant use of real estate, too. Happily, grapes like poor soil. "It is fortunate for mankind that the vine thrives on soil that is little good for anything else," self-sufficiency pioneer John Seymour wrote in *The Self-Sufficient Gardener*. With a bit of elbow grease, even vacant lots can be put to use.

In Morningside, Detroit, for example, the community and nonprofits have worked with local winery Detroit Vineyards to plant 1,000 vines in empty lots. When these cold-hardy red Marquette grapes are eventually pressed, the wine's terroir (the French term used to describe all environmental factors that influence a wine) will reflect Detroit's lakeside climate, frequent fogs and heavy, alkaline soils—as well as its social fabric, like the local knowledge of the growers digging down through the city's concrete layers.

Even the most populous cities can be home to vineyards. In 1930s Paris, residents created the Clos Montmartre vineyard in order to block a real estate project—its deep-blue grapes are still harvested annually by the city. In 2013, inspired by time spent in Paris, winemaker Elly Hartshorn convinced San Francisco's Recreation & Parks Department to let locals grow on vacant parkland. These growers are seizing space wherever it presents itself, and creating wines that sum up the distinct flavors of their city.
Words by Stevie Mackenzie-Smith

Left Photograph: Marcus Schäfer / Trunk Archive. Right Photograph: Piczo

Golden Rules

A taxonomy of obedience.

Rules that seem ridiculous to you may make perfect sense to the person that made them. And if people don't follow the rules set out—in a relationship, at work or during a global pandemic—well, frustration is understandable. Whether you're tightly laced or laissez-faire, the path to harmony is understanding what rules and rule-breaking are really about, and why. Cross-cultural psychologist Michele Gelfand's book *Rule Makers, Rule Breakers* covers just that, describing "tightness" and "looseness" as an approach to rules and a way to view the world. She believes that both flagrant rule-flouting and draconian diktats can be understood and overcome with empathy and negotiation. *Interview by Bella Gladman*

BG: *What's the basic idea behind "tight" and "loose" cultures?* **MG:** As humans, we judge others based on our own cultural lenses. Some groups have a tight mindset and desire order, while groups with a loose mindset don't notice rules as much, and are more comfortable with ambiguity. Both positions provide different advantages. Tight groups, whether nation-states, organizations or households, tend to have a lot of coordination and self-control. Our research shows they tend to have less debt and alcoholism. Loose cultures, on the other hand, struggle with self-regulation, but they are open, tolerant and creative. These differences create conflict. The key is diagnosis—figuring out where you fall on the tight-loose spectrum and why, then looking at the people around you, and empathizing with them about why they might be there.

BG: *What affects whether you're tight or loose?* **MG:** When you have a lot of threat, whether it's individual hardship, or on a national level—such as pandemics, natural disasters or invasions—you need stricter rules to coordinate, ergo you become tighter. It's a basic evolutionary adaption. In a looser context, there is less threat, generally speaking, so you can afford to be permissive.

BG: *In the time of COVID-19, how can we get people to follow rules?* **MG:** The pandemic means we're under threat and we need to tighten. Strong leadership and consistent messaging helps people to understand that the threat is real: It's really hard to tighten from the bottom up in a looser culture, and trying to shame people into doing things is not effective—it's a norm violation in itself.

BG: *What's the best way to negotiate across a tight-loose divide?* **MG:** All cultures have tight and loose elements simultaneously, and for individuals, it's the same principle. Rank the different areas that need coordination, in terms of what's most important for you to maintain tightness or looseness around. If you're raising kids, that might be bedtimes, curfews and messiness. Which ones need to be tight? Which ones can be looser? Of course, you all have to agree, but you'll benefit from tolerance and less irritation.

BG: *Can opposing positions be a positive thing?* **MG:** We need both "order" and "openness" people in the same space—their strengths are our liabilities, and vice versa. You could even think about being with someone on the other side of the tight-loose spectrum as a gift—you have someone that helps you with that balance. Maybe you start appreciating that person's tightness! Maybe it's not about trying to change them but, after negotiating, trying to appreciate what they bring to the table.

In November 2020, a team of British researchers found that personality traits accounted for a third of the variation in an individual's compliance with social distancing regulations. They suggested using surveys on social media to gauge personality types, and then tailoring health messaging accordingly.

Historically, people have filled their homes with an assortment of objects that are both practical and personal: vinyl records, CDs, DVDs, books and photo albums. Today, as most of these taste signifiers have come to be consumed and stored digitally, more fluid, temporary interior design objects have swept in to fill the gap. Depending on your tastes, these might include rose-gold pineapples, drink trolleys, a bust sculpture, tiny vases or display trays—objects that don't reveal personal preferences but rather convey identity based on in-group status. They're objects that say, *I'm in on the trend*, while also, crucially, being swappable, as both trends and personal desires change.

"There's something interesting about the home being a space you actively 'edit,' with changeable, updatable vignettes, a constant work in progress," says Antonia Ward, global director of advisory services at Stylus, a trend-forecasting agency. She chalks it up to the "Instagrammification of our habits and habitats" in which "you can curate a corner of a room and photograph it... no one need see the terrible piles of laundry just out of shot." [1]

But today's "editable" objects, in many ways, serve the same purpose as the Victorian pinned butterflies or CD towers of yesteryear: They provide memories into which we might dip. The difference is these memories aren't necessarily our own. "We are very quick to add nostalgia these days, including *fauxstalgia*, which is the nostalgia for a past you didn't even experience," says Ward. With all those knockoff Eames chairs and plywood credenzas waiting for us on Wayfair, we can so easily join the throngs who want to live the mid-century-modern life, despite having been born well after the mid-century. We're also not hemmed in by what we might buy based on where we've been. Persian rugs don't have to come from Iran; they can come from Amazon. Turkish tea sets can be bought on Etsy. We can order anything we like, which means we can curate memories without experiencing them. [2]

A few "collectible," personal objects remain popular. Books, especially, continue to exist as status symbols and as repositories of memories. There have been some trends that reconfigured their presentation—for example, turning them so the spines face the wall. But this suggestion, advanced by Instagram interiors bloggers, was widely received with ridicule for robbing our homes of one of the few personal, physical items left. According to Ward, the showcasing of books implies, "'Maybe I will read this again'; 'One day I might look something up'; 'I might lend this to someone'; 'I'm hoping to finally cook that complicated recipe.'"

Ultimately, the objects we display are portals to all sorts of imagined realms. They "can be used as totems or touchstones to draw you into a story, to transport you to another time or place through the locus of that object," wrote Alexis Lloyd, a product designer, in *The Atlantic*. While even a rose-gold pineapple can be, perhaps, personally meaningful, what happens to the attached memories when you toss it for the next trendy thing?

Words by Cody Delistraty

NOTES

1. The increased number of people who rent rather than own property has contributed to the boom in design objects. According to market research firm Mintel, whereas homeowners invest in big-ticket items, such as sofas, renters spend their disposable income on small objects that can travel with them.

2. The ability to source near-identical objects has contributed to the global homogenization of interior design. In an influential 2016 essay for *The Verge*, writer Kyle Chayka coined the term "AirSpace" to refer to the eerily similar style of hospitality ventures around the world.
—

ON BOREDOM

by Pip Usher

In *Diary of a Cosmonaut: 211 Days in Space*, Valentin Lebedev recorded his daily experiences during a record-breaking seven-month stint in space. Even as scientific experiments occupied his time, the monotony crept in; as he noted in his diary after only a week, "the drab routine has begun." Boredom, it turns out, can affect anyone—including Soviet cosmonauts. Characterized by feelings of emptiness, frustration and apathy, it is widely recognized as a temporary emotional state that arises in response to tedium.

For some, the result can be impulsive behaviors with negative consequences, such as gambling and drug abuse. Others may find themselves mindlessly scrolling through their apps in what has been dubbed "phone boredom." Yet a growing number of psychologists are warning against our efforts to do away with boredom. A lack of external stimulus can encourage creativity, improve self-control and serve as motivation to pursue new goals.

Scientists living on remote bases in Antarctica fill their calendars with a lively variety of social events, from talent shows and skits to holiday celebrations. The same was true last century for explorer Ernest Shackleton, who packed a small printing press on one expedition to keep his crew entertained. The issue for Lebedev, it seems, may not have been the ennui itself. Rather, he simply didn't know what to do with it. *Photograph by Fanny Latour-Lambert*

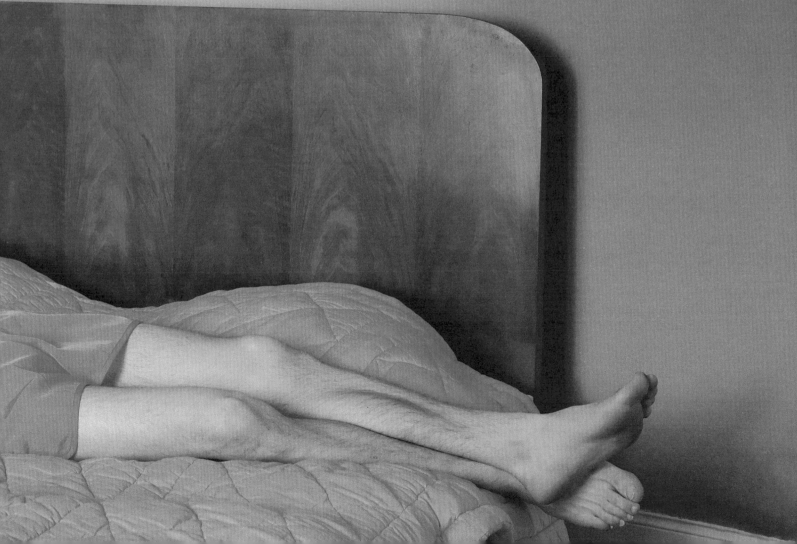

The Next Big Nothing

On not quite making it.

Fans of the TV show *Gilmore Girls* waited nine years after the end of the original series to find out what became of its precocious co-lead, Rory Gilmore. Throughout the first seven seasons of the show, Rory's narrative is that she is destined for greatness. In the four-part coda, she moves back to her hometown after being fired from a job, and rekindles a romance with her now-engaged college boyfriend. With one (frequently mentioned) article for *The New Yorker* under her belt, she starts to edit the local newspaper, all the while insisting she won't be in town long enough to join the local "30-Something Gang."

There are, surely, many real-world examples of people who were the next big thing—until they no longer were. Remember that super-talented band from school who once had their single played on the radio? Or the guy from the next town who was being scouted by a sports agent? These stories might briefly attain the status of local folklore, but the only people who keep clinging to them are the ones who didn't make it. If you achieve renown, there's no reason to dwell on the moments before it happened. Only those who have success snatched away have cause to be nostalgic about the moments they were on the verge of it.

We tend to think of "might-have-beens" with pity—not because there's anything shameful about trying and failing, but because it's more painful and embarrassing to fall from a height than to just trip over something. They are also an uncomfortable reminder of the hollowness of our society's emphasis on individual accomplishments as a marker of personal value, and the promise that "you can achieve anything you set your mind to"—something only true for the exceptional few.

Still, there's something in the notion of never giving up on your dreams, not because they're necessarily within reach but because the moments of ecstatic anticipation before a reward are as much a part of the human experience as the payoff. Those who never made it can live forever with that joy, without ever finding out if a goal was worth it.
Words by Debika Ray

BUBBLE LANGUAGE
by Pip Usher

In a world governed by grown-ups, kids need their own identity. Bubble language—a vernacular that adds suffixes to the end of English words to disguise them—is a handy technique. Some bubble languages, like Pig Latin, are widely known; others are unique byproducts of a certain school or social circle. The guiding principle, though, is always the same: To the uninitiated, it should sound like utter gibberish. Because bubble language is both secretive in its rules and selective about whom it admits, it has the added benefit of bonding its speakers together. As the name suggests, they exist in a bubble together—and the outside world of adults isn't welcome.

Forever Young

Photograph: Luc Braquet

The ageless appeal of child stars.

In 2015, podcaster Jonathan Goldstein produced a segment for *Reply All* which asked the question: *Why Is Mason Reese Crying?* Reese was a ubiquitous 1970s presence on American television, cropping up on talk shows and in commercials of every kind. He was a striking, unusual looking child with distinctive facial features and bright red hair and the preternaturally adult demeanor and quick-fire banter common to many child stars.

Goldstein tracked Reese down to ask him about a time when he was co-hosting the popular *Mike Douglas Show* as a child. On the podcast, Goldstein describes a YouTube video where Reese's precocious facade crumbles dramatically with inexplicable emotion over Harry Chapin's live performance of "Cat's in the Cradle." The little boy abruptly abandons his formerly frivolous tone, to the visible discomfort of Douglas, and instead turns to the side, hiding his face and heaving with inconsolable sobs. It's a bizarre, unsettling moment. There is something about it that crystallizes the queasy relationship we have to child stars. We revel in their performance of incongruent, miniaturized maturity, and then are aghast when the reality of their youth is suddenly revealed too overtly—as though it wasn't there for us to see all along.

People find it deeply compelling to see Reese as an adult, which is true of all child actors, whether they continued their success as adults or not. We are lured in by clickbait at the bottom of trashy websites—a picture of some formerly adorable actor is accompanied by the promise that we won't believe how they look now. Haley Joel Osment suffers particularly from this: Hoards of unkind strangers are ever eager to crow over how the features we knew from his iconic roles in *The Sixth Sense* and *A.I.* are still visible, are still resolutely themselves, but are receding into his broadening face.

Of course, this happens to all of us as we age, but, I think, there is a certain sense of glee when we get the chance to react with derision. A part of us is glad to sneer at these people who seemed to have so much, so early on—the striking obscenity of a pint-size millionaire, the wrongness of a child with so much power. But if they won big early on, they paid for it later: Their burden is to always reflect our horror of mortality back to us, endlessly fascinating us, revealing too starkly what we lose when we lose our childhood.
Words by Megan Nolan

Botched Beauty

When fine art gets in a fix.

In 2012, the art world gasped in horror when a disastrously amateur restoration of Elías García Martínez's fresco of Christ in agony, *Ecce Homo*, came out looking like a cross between a pained potato and a frilled monkey. But the furor quickly turned to delight. People worldwide cheerfully renamed the image *Ecce Mono* ("Behold the monkey"), or pasted the same potato face on the *Mona Lisa*, *The Scream* and the entire cast of *The Last Supper*. The DIY restorer, 81-year-old Cecilia Giménez, became famous, and her town of Borja, Spain became a destination. Hundreds of thousands of visitors have visited over the last eight years, hoping to see Giménez's simian Jesus. Adding to the fun, American composer Paul Fowler and librettist Andrew Flack produced a comic opera about the event, *Behold the Man, La Ópera de Cecilia*, which debuted to an audience of 700 in Borja in 2016.

As shocking as this botched restoration was, it wasn't the first and it won't be the last. In Spain alone, where there is little regulation concerning who may engage in such work, amateur painters have inadvertently made several serious artworks laughable over the last few years. There's been a cartoonish repainting of a 16th-century sculpture of St. George, the garish recoloration of two 18th-century statues of the holy family, and this past summer, an astoundingly naive reinterpretation of Mary's face on a 17th-century painting of the Immaculate Conception.[1]

Although each of these elicited well-justified anger among art historians and professional restorers, it is hard not to find them amusing. This isn't the smirking condescension of schadenfreude. It is a more benign, self-reflective pleasure, because every amateur, every weekend DIY artisan can identify with the wide gap that often opens between vision and execution. We understand that, for most of us, botched jobs are part of the process, despite our aspirations. In fact, they are a crucial part of handiwork.

David Pye, a British professor of furniture design, identified high-quality craft with the "workmanship of risk," in which "the quality of the result is not predetermined but depends on the judgement, dexterity and care which the maker exercises." The possibility of failure makes the work worthwhile. Usually, though, our failures don't see much light; we throw them away, redo them or resign ourselves to live quietly with them. But when a spectacularly botched job captures the world's attention, it is humorous because *that could have been me.*[2] The lapse in judgment, the slip of dexterity, the incautious result all seem charmingly familiar.

Words by Alex Anderson

NOTES

1. In November 2020, Spanish conservation experts once again expressed their dismay at the country's lax approach to restorations after a statue of a woman's bust in Palencia emerged from restoration work only to draw comparisons to a "potato head."
—
—

2. It is often the case that we connect with ancient art through its relatable oddities rather than its overwhelming beauty, perhaps because strange details help humanize the long-dead artist. For example, Tuscany's medieval fresco *The Tree of Fertility* (pictured right) has become famous for the unusual fruit it bears.

Photograph: Niccolò Caranti. *The Tree of Fertility*, Massa Marittima

Dearly Departed

A note on obituaries.

Having an obituary written about you is a sign that you have lived a life of note. You might have done or experienced a variety of things to reach those pages: received a significant award, died in battle, raised notable sums for the local hospice, or massacred one's own people. Still, the only way to have an obituary published is to have died, just like everybody else before you.

Remembering is distinct from memorializing. In the immediate days or weeks after a non-celebrity's death, local obituary writers search for the facts. This approach is perhaps even helpful to the reader: Who should be referenced in a With Sympathy card? Is there a request for flowers, or charity donations? It is only once the reach of a life has been noted that its impact might then be assessed. Mourners require time to judge how to honor a person's legacy, be that through fundraising or by heeding a cautionary tale. On the other hand, obituaries of the famous are rangy and ambitious; they help establish the context in which an individual came to prominence. Instead of finding the name of the funeral home in the obituary, we find clues to what our society fears or reveres.

A small handful of obituary writers have made it their mission to equalize this written record of the dead. Jim Nicholson, for example, began writing obituaries for the *Philadelphia Daily News* in 1982. He'd previously been an investigative reporter, but he devoted 19 years of his career to writing what would be, for many of his subjects, the first and last words about them in print. Nicholson's obituaries were notable not for their form, but for their content. He wrote about ordinary people—those who cooked and cleaned and transported their neighbors for a living—with the same tone he would use for celebrities, academics, activists and politicians. Because in the end, whether the obituary is about a movie star or a high school teacher, it means the same thing: A person is born, lives and is affected by others, and in turn, affects those around them. They leave but are not forgotten.
Words by Salome Wagaine

2.

Features

PIERRE YOVANO—VITCH:

A CHÂTEAU FIT FOR DESIGN *ROYALTY*.

Pierre Yovanovitch's ultimate design showroom is also his home of more than a decade. *Annick Weber* meets the man with the keys to the castle. Photography by *Romain Laprade*

Although he spent years renovating every corner of the sprawling Château de Fabrègues, Pierre Yovanovitch's favorite thing about his country house is not actually its interior. When at home in the South of France, the designer likes to spend most of his time outdoors. More days than not, he starts his mornings taking his three sheepdogs for a walk around the grounds, past the small, free-standing chapel and through the Louis Benech–designed yew labyrinth. He will pop out again later to feed the chickens or do bits of gardening. "I'm mostly a nervous person, but in my garden I'm calm," he says, speaking over a video call from his home office, which overlooks the estate. "It's where I get to disconnect and be a dreamer."

With his studio working on 40 active projects across Europe and the US, Yovanovitch is a man in need of relaxation. When we speak, the 55-year-old is fresh off the Eurostar train from London, where his firm is currently renovating a townhouse. For someone who regularly commutes between his headquarters in Paris, New York (where he also has offices) and the house in Provence, he's looking surprisingly fresh-faced, wearing chunky glasses that recall a 1970s Yves Saint Laurent. Since establishing his studio in 2001, Yovanovitch has completed countless private residences, as well as interiors for hotels, restaurants, art galleries, offices and boutiques for the likes of Michelin-starred chef Hélène Darroze, billionaire businessman François-Henri Pinault and footwear designer Christian Louboutin. His resolutely contemporary style—blending a purist sensibility, site-specific art, and bespoke and vintage furniture—has made him a key player in a new French design aesthetic, defined not by ornate adornment, but by understated luxury.

Yovanovitch found his way to design via high-end fashion. After graduating from business school, he started his career in the early 1990s working with Pierre Cardin on menswear. "They were very formative years," he says. "Cardin was a master of volume and proportion. He told stories through his clothing." Though he was given more and more design responsibility during his eight years at the company, Yovanovitch realized that he belonged to a different world. "The creative process made me remember how I was constantly drawing apartment layouts in my imagination as a child," he says, a statement which

conjures the image of Yovanovitch sketching blueprints in the sandbox where others played. "I loved working closely with Cardin, but in the end, my passion was elsewhere. His approach is still alive in my work today though: He greatly influenced the way I think about symmetry and silhouette. You can make someone look taller or shorter depending on the cut, color and shape of a dress. I think you can do the same with a space." While he found that the similarities between the two disciplines were many, Yovanovitch had to get his head around a few changes. "Fashion gives you more flexibility to create," he explains. "A dress is worn for one or two years, but a home should last a long time."

In the 20 years since founding his interior architecture practice, Yovanovitch has never fully let go of his background in couture. He has become celebrated for applying the same tailor-made approach to interiors that a fashion designer brings to dressmaking. Like a couturier drawing on a network of embroiderers, lace makers and pattern-cutters, Yovanovitch relies on the savoir-faire of the dozens of craftspeople his firm regularly collaborates with. "They've become something like a family," he says. "I've been working with the same woodworker, ceramicist and glassblower for 15 years. Each one of them is an expert in turning simple materials into long-lasting pieces." When he was tasked with transforming a ramshackle Douro Valley winery into the chic Quinta da Côrte guesthouse in 2018, Yovanovitch got together a team of local experts to help create a decidedly Portuguese space complete with azulejo tiles, white adobe walls and hand-painted frescoes. "I wanted guests to be able to feel where they are," he says. It is, of course, a costly and time-consuming way of working; the Yovanovitch method is not designed to scale up.

As much as his work gives center stage to the best of contemporary craftsmanship, there's a reverence for the past, particularly in the use of vintage 20th-century furniture. Yovanovitch is an avid collector of the Swedish Grace movement, a 1920s art deco offshoot that he came to discover when designing the scenography for an exhibition on one of its lead designers, Axel Einar Hjorth. Almost all of his projects incorporate Scandinavian design pieces, such as Einar Hjorth pinewood rocking chairs, Paavo Tynell lamps and Gunnar Asplund dining chairs. Even OOPS, Yovanovitch's debut furniture collection with its teddy bear-eared armchairs, contains subtle nods to the soft, sheepskin-covered loungers designed in the 1930s by Viggo Boesen. "These names are mostly unfamiliar to collectors," he says of his affinity for lesser-known Scandinavian designers. "As soon as I start a commission, I also start looking for the right furniture at auction houses and antique dealers. Good pieces are hard to come by, so it's not something that I can leave until the end." The same goes for the art he chooses for interiors. He favors yet-to-be-discovered talents such as Claire Tabouret and Wilhelm Sasnal over the Damien Hirsts of contemporary art.

The one project that brings together all of Yovanovitch's craftspeople, favorite artists and furniture designers is the 8,600-square-foot Château de Fabrègues—his "life project." When he first came across the Provençal château in a real estate ad in a magazine in 2009, though, buying a country house was the last thing on his mind. Having grown up in nearby Nice, he went to visit it out of professional curiosity. "The structure was completely run down, but I was drawn to the simplicity of its 17th-century architecture," he explains. "Unlike the grand châteaux of the 18th century, there was very little ornamentation as people were poorer, which allowed me to freely readapt the decor to my liking." Over the course of the extensive three-year renovations, Yovanovitch and his team of artisans created a sober, at times monastic home. Hints of the past remain throughout, from the original limestone floors to the sculpted ceilings, meticulously restored by Yovanovitch's go-to

Left: Sideboard, table and chairs by Christen Emanuel Kjœr Monberg, 1923; *Frau vor goldenhem Hintergrund* artwork by Stephan Balkenhol, 2009; ceiling light by Paavo Tynell, circa 1948; lamp by Atelier Stiffel, circa 1950; ceramics by Robert Picault, circa 1960; candelabrum by Tommi Parzinger, circa 1940.

*"I want to change things all the time... I have sleepless nights
where I think about the space, the light and where a particular chair should sit."*

Yovanovitch's château is home to a collection of art that includes works by both established and upcoming artists, such as Stephen Balkenhol, Georg Baselitz, Claire Tabouret, Jeremy Demester and Valentin Carron.

plasterer, Joël Puisais. "My role is like that of a *chef d'orchestre*, conducting an orchestra of very different, but equally passionate talent," he says.

Despite the pared-back feel of the overall design, the château is studded with eclectic touches. In the living room, pieces from different countries and centuries are put into dialogue with one another: Custom-made linen sofas rub shoulders with a Swedish Grace oak banquette, and a period stucco fireplace complements one of Francesco Clemente's jigsaw-like watercolors. It's an unexpected mix, but it makes the place feel lived-in and real. With every nook and cranny curated down to the smallest detail, was Yovanovitch worried his house would end up looking like a showroom? "*Non, non,* not at all," he says. "It's a happy house with all my favorite things in it, a place that lives and gets messy from time to time. We like to cook and eat, sometimes we dance. It reflects my personality more than anything else."

Château de Fabrègues wouldn't be the home it is without Yovanovitch's contemporary art collection. Inside are pieces by American sculptor Richard Nonas and Franco-Chinese painter Yan Pei-Ming, while the garden is host to an Alicja Kwade installation inspired by the planetary system. The work he's perhaps fondest of is a Claire Tabouret fresco, which covers the entire château chapel and took a month to complete. "When you walk inside the chapel, you have this mural with 85 children looking directly at you, it's very powerful," he says.

What makes Château de Fabrègues different from Yovanovitch's other projects is that it will never be fully completed. Whereas client commissions are typically wrapped up the moment keys are handed over, designing his own home is an ongoing process. With no timelines or cut-off dates, he says it's impossible to draw a line under the vast project—particularly when you're a perfectionist. "I want to change things all the time, repaint a room or move furniture around," he explains. "I have sleepless nights where I think about the space, the light and where a particular chair should sit. I already had that as a teenager: I wouldn't be able to sleep unless the furniture around me in my bedroom was arranged right. I've always been obsessed with beauty surrounding me." As an autodidact with a keen interest in the arts but no formal design education, he follows his intuition rather than movements or trends. "I think I'm freer to do what I want than most qualified designers," he says. He believes that he owes much of his style to this greater sense of freedom. Steering away from flashy pretensions, Yovanovitch's specialty lies in crafting harmonious volumes smoothed by soft lines and natural materials.

If there's one thing that has changed in his practice over the years, it's the use of color. He has moved on from the white minimalism of his early days. At Château de Fabrègues, the largely neutral palette is punctuated with playful accents of yellow, petrol blue and brown to underline the architectural scale. True to his made-to-measure approach, he creates custom tints for each project, never buying ready-mixed paint. "I'm a child of the South after all," he says with a smile. "We like light, color and fun. I've come

to realize that adding pops of color helps to make the architecture more interesting, rather than distracting from it." In his 2019 redesign of the Villa Noailles gift shop, it seems as though he has reconnected with his Southern French roots more than ever before. Located on the Côte d'Azur in a Robert Mallet-Stevens–designed building, the art center's boutique now features peachy orange ceilings and a mix of sunshine yellow, turquoise and terra-cotta red walls, purposefully clashing with splashes of electric blue in stark contrast to the white cubist exterior.

Be it in the form of bold color accents or eclectic furniture pairings, moments of drama have become more frequent in Yovanovitch's recent work. His tendency to at times dramatize interiors is a nod to his passion for opera and set design, which he cites as major inspirations. "Opera sets are at their most powerful when they reflect the soul of the work, its music and characters," he explains. "I want to do the same in my oeuvre. With each space, I want to tell a new story—a story that fits my client and the locale."

Fittingly, Yovanovitch has recently landed a commission to design the set for a production of Verdi's 1851 opera *Rigoletto* in Basel: "It's a dream come true," he says. "I've always been a firm believer that if you really want something, then one day you'll get it." As one would expect, Yovanovitch is planning on a design that respects the soul of the oeuvre, while making it relevant for 21st-century audiences. In this way, it's not unlike what he did at Château de Fabrègues: combining the ancient and the modern to craft a work of timeless beauty.

FEATURES

EVA 58

Photography by Emma Trim & Styling by Dominick Barcelona

Nathan Ma meets Eva Victor: the character comedian changing her industry without leaving her apartment.

> *"I have all this pent-up fear and fraudulence
> and worry about not living up to the titles assigned to me."*

On Twitter, comedian Eva Victor is a headline act. As an actor, her on-camera credits include Showtime's prestige drama *Billions*. As a writer, her satirical pieces have been published on *Reductress* and in *The New Yorker*. But Victor has found her beat in short-form comedy sketches that she films with her phone and uploads to Twitter. The videos are low-fi and low-to no-budget, like Instagram Stories with a plot. In one, she plays a glamorous widow, idly cooperating with the police as they investigate the disappearance of her husband who she *definitely* did not kill. In the next, she's a record store clerk with a septum piercing and plenty of attitude: The girl in a movie who is "different."

In these videos, Victor doesn't assume the role of different people—she fully inhabits them. Her humor comes in two acts: First,

she recreates familiar characters—often Hollywood tropes or metropolitan millennials—with eerie precision and an unforgiving eye for detail. Then, she knowingly exposes the unspoken fault lines under each of her impressions. Her record store clerk character, for example, gets dumped by the high-school quarterback two weeks after prom—a rebuttal to the happy endings we have grown to expect.

When Victor logs onto Zoom, she's sitting cross-legged on the floor with a kale sandwich on her plate in front of a massive, four-door fridge. At 26 years old, she has just got the keys to a new apartment in New York. The walls are bare and the space is mostly unfurnished—it's a blank canvas for her next act.

NM: *What's it like to work as a comedian in a pandemic?* **EV:** It's a

weird task, but it also serves as an escape—not even doing comedy, but writing at all. These people don't exist, but they get to go to a party and they get to go to a store and whatever else that I can't [in a pandemic].

NM: *You recently finished a screenplay. What catalyzed your move from on-camera work toward on-paper work?* **EV:** As much as my work lives on phones right now, I really don't like having a phone. Writing takes you away from the noise, even if it's for an hour or two. I was a playwriting minor in college, and wrote a few—I must say—horrible plays. Still, I loved the quiet practice of that. Returning to that private work is exciting. I also like that when something is on paper you can hold it in your hand: "I made this! Look, it's on a piece of paper so it must be real."

NM: *How have you been spending your time outside of work?* **EV:** I'm about to start a pottery class, which I've been looking forward to for a long time. I've also been jogging—horribly, I look like a little duck. It's like trying to outrun your thoughts, in a way that makes you shut your brain down—because your brain *will* kill you. When I was in high school, I had my first bout of depression in a big way, and it was really scary and I thought I was gonna die. Now it happens every so often, like my period: "Okay, it's here, it's gonna go, it's gonna come back, let's just live with it."

NM: *What makes you laugh?* **EV:** I really like silly people. Should I just name them? The Michelle Buteau Netflix special is so funny, and *Pen15* too. I also thought *Rosemary's Baby* was funny—like, I think it's funny when we talk

Victor wears a jumpsuit by PH5
and a shirt by Uniqlo.

FEATURES

about death, or wanting to die, because it makes me feel connected. Take *I May Destroy You.* It's taking me a while to finish it but it's so worth it. It's triggering, and it's accurate in terms of the experience of trauma, and that is satisfying. It's the first time, actually, that I've felt like I've seen something depict what that particular experience of trauma felt like in my life in a way that really landed and hurt my feelings too. That hit me really hard, but in a good way. Like it was meant to.

NM: *Forms of creative expression are implicated in the same power structures as our lives in general. You deal with these power structures in your comedy, like with your character of the overeager girlfriend telling her boyfriend about why she wants to go to "straight pride." What inspired those parodies?* **EV:** Maybe a year and a half ago, Alyssa Milano was like, "Women, we're on a sex strike!" and everyone was like, "No, we're not. That doesn't serve us in anyway. We like sex." People are so fucking insane and they have really roundabout

ways of doing what they want. People organizing a straight pride? I was like, "This is funny, this is really funny, but stupid, and you're not getting what you want from this. I'm gonna make it harder for you to get what you want."

NM: *There are also plenty of opportunities to compare yourself to those around you. How do you feel about competitiveness in comedy?* **EV:** I'm so grateful that so many people are so funny! And sometimes I'm like, "Wow, I'm incredibly funny," but it has nothing to do with anyone else. There's no limit to what people need as entertainment to survive. Whenever people get an opportunity to make what they want to make, it's brilliant and it's golden. I think all of our favorite TV shows are just people being like, "I want to fucking make this. This is my dream, and it's exciting to me, and it sounds funny." All these rules are put in place, but I don't think those formulas are necessarily helpful.

NM: *People who follow you on social media generally see you when*

you're in character. Who is the real Eva Victor? **EV:** Oh, God, don't ask me. I don't know. If I think about that for too long, I'll explode or die. It's weird. I still have trouble saying I'm a writer, even when I'm getting paid to write, which is a pretty justifiable reason to say that. And when I came out, I was like, "I'm bi and everyone needs to remember that," but I think after a few years of living in myself longer, I'm like, "Oh, God, please don't hold me to anything I say in terms of who I am." [When it comes to my sexuality] we can put things under "queer" and you can hold onto that. Mom, you can look that word up.

I don't feel like anyone really asks me to say "I'm a writer," "I'm a comedian," "I'm an actor" and I'm so glad that I don't have those titles because I think I have all this pent-up fear and fraudulence and worry about not living up to the titles assigned to me. I don't like that and all that fear—all that pressure—is coming from me. I guess I'm, like, the one that just got an apartment. And a sandwich.

Left: Victor wears a jumpsuit by PH5 and a shirt by Uniqlo. Above Right: She wears a coat by Helmut Lang and a vest by Perry Ellis. Below Right: She wears a cardigan and trousers by Leset.

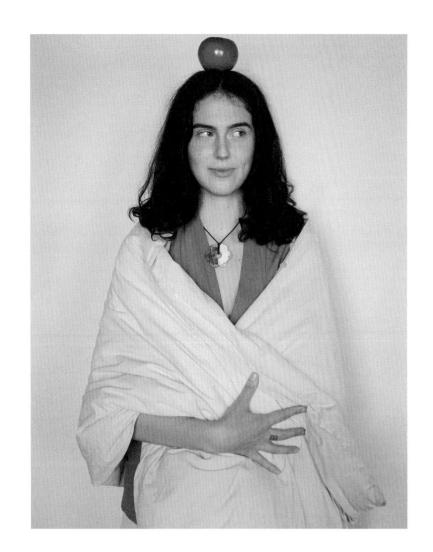

Archive:
Jean Stein

Jean Stein brought the world to her Upper West Side apartment, then transformed her guests' party anecdotes into stirring oral histories of the American dream. *Annick Weber* chronicles the life of one of New York's great storytellers.

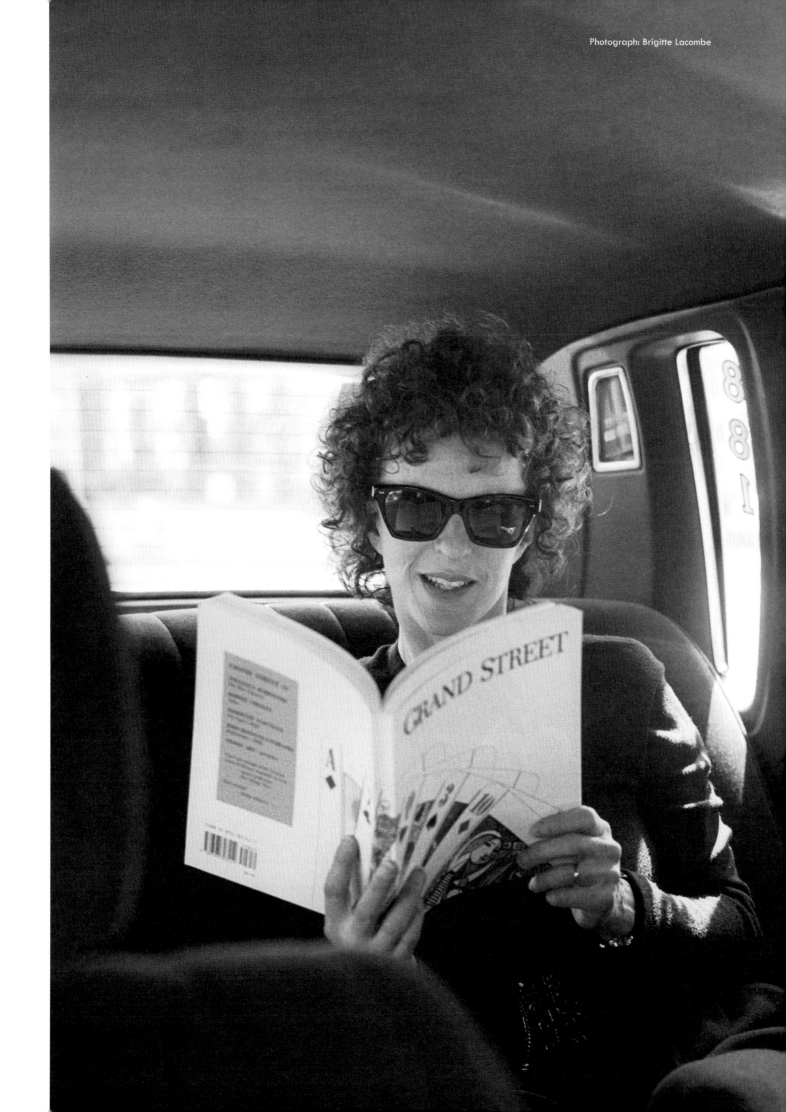

The first thing that many people noticed about Jean Stein was the tape recorder. Though clunky and somewhat old-fashioned-looking, it served her well on decades' worth of trips across America, during which she interviewed subjects as varied as the topics she covered. Stein was not an ordinary writer for whom a notepad and pen would likely have sufficed; she was a master of the oral history form, and the tape recorder was essential in fully capturing and collecting her interviewees' firsthand accounts of modern American life.

"She found the métier she loved in conducting interviews," Stein's daughter, Katrina vanden Heuvel, says, speaking on the phone from New York City. "She seemed quiet and vulnerable with her shy, fluttery voice, but she was fearless with the tape recorder. She was a relentless interviewer and a beautiful listener, who would wait until she got exactly what she wanted to hear from her subjects." The cassette recordings, combined with Stein's restless curiosity, laid the foundations for comprehensive oral histories about the assassinated US attorney general Robert F. Kennedy (*American Journey*, published in 1970), the Andy

Warhol muse Edie Sedgwick (*Edie*, published in 1982) and a group of Angelenos who shaped the face of their city (*West of Eden*, published in 2016). Her oeuvre spanned politics to the underground art scene, both of which she was involved in, but never fully a part of. "She was able to see milieus that she wouldn't have seen, had she not had that tape recorder," vanden Heuvel tells me. "Essentially, it was a way of getting out of where she was born."

A daughter of Hollywood royalty, Stein grew up in a bubble. When she was three, in 1937, her family moved from Chicago to a sprawling mansion in Beverly Hills. The relocation allowed her father, Jules—a conservative Republican and ophthalmologist-turned-entertainment magnate—to be closer to the glitz and glamor of Hollywood, where the new headquarters of his music booking agency, MCA, was based. The family mansion quickly became legendary for its parties, where Los Angeles' film, music and theater set gathered to pay court to the powerful patriarch. Stein liked to describe her childhood home as a "fantasy," remembering with regret how she and her sister were "brought down to curtsy like little dolls in our dressing gowns" before being tucked into bed by their nannies. Life in La-La Land could have given her all the wealth and security she wanted, but Stein—a fervent Democrat—chose to venture out and see more of the world.

From a young age, Stein attended schools in San Francisco, Switzerland, New York and Massachusetts, before enrolling at Paris' Sorbonne university in the mid-

Left Photograph: © Inge Morath / Magnum Photos / Scanpix. Right Photograph: Brigitte Lacombe

"She was able to see milieus that she wouldn't
have seen, had she not had that tape recorder. Essentially, it was a way of
getting out of where she was born."

1950s. It was in the French capital that she made her initial forays not only into the art of interviewing, but also the world's intellectual circles. The first major commission she landed was an interview for *The Paris Review* with William Faulkner, with whom she was having an affair. Impressed by her direct, even blunt interview style, the literary magazine kept her on as an assistant to the founding editor, George Plimpton, a role she held for several years before moving back to New York. (Plimpton remained a close friend of Stein's and went on to edit her books *American Journey* and *Edie*.) "She made her great mark at *The Paris Review*, which informed her later on when she was working on *Grand Street*," vanden Heuvel says, referring to the literary and visual arts magazine Stein edited from 1990 to 2004. "She was a great editor, always looking for the new, the vibrant, the interesting. That too was almost oral history; *Grand Street* was a place where she could make various voices heard."

In her personal life, Stein enjoyed doing what she did professionally as an editor and an oral historian: bringing together a mix of people from all sorts of backgrounds. She was a passionate host with an eclectic group of friends. As she told the *Los Angeles Times* in 1990: "I am very interested in these different worlds coming together. In a way, I've lived my life in New York that way." At the parties held starting in the early 1960s at her Upper West Side apartment, one was as likely to run into No-

bel laureates and diplomats as civil rights activists, dissident poets and avant-garde artists.

Among the invitees were Jackie Kennedy Onassis and members of the Black Panther party, Andy Warhol in the company of his Factory pals, and Norman Mailer exchanging punches with Gore Vidal. And in the midst of it all was Stein, observing, orchestrating and connecting her guests with effortless ability. "She was the ringmaster," the Pulitzer Prize–winning cartoonist Jules Feiffer said in *The New York Times'* obituary for Stein. "Her demeanor was quiet, but she was noticeable in a room. She was the centerpiece without commanding attention." It was this lack of pretense that her friends admired the most in her. Stein invited people not for their fame, but because they were unafraid to live life on their own terms.

Out of the three oral histories she wrote, the one she was most fond of was *Edie*. Edie Sedgwick, unsurprisingly, was a friend of Stein's. Aware of Sedgwick's anorexia and drug abuse years before her death from an overdose in 1971, Stein put her up in her daughter Wendy's bedroom in 1967 after Sedgwick accidentally set fire to her room at the Chelsea Hotel. The sisterly devotion with which Stein looked after Sedgwick stemmed to some extent from her own familiarity with the perils of high society: Like Stein, Sedgwick was born into great wealth as the daughter of New England patricians.

Edie allowed Stein to explore what drove her protagonist's downfall from aristocratic heiress to doomed superstar. She spent multiple years interviewing and reinterviewing Sedgwick's family and friends to paint a full picture of her subject's short life, but also of a 1960s America fascinated with youth, beauty and stardom. The illusory nature of the American dream was a recurring topic in Stein's work, becoming the basis for her final book, *West of Eden*, in which she recorded the nation's "trickster promise" through interviews with five of Los Angeles' most influential families, including her own, compiled over more than 20 years.

Stein died by suicide on April 30, 2017 at the age of 83, leaving behind countless unpublished oral histories, including records of the 1992 Los Angeles riots and Havana on the eve of the Cuban revolution. With age, her social circles had become increasingly smaller. "She had a hard time because so many of her friends passed away," vanden Heuvel tells me of her mother's death. "She stopped having parties and instead started seeing people one-on-one. But she missed it." In her breakthrough 1955 interview with Faulkner, Stein asked him what he thought the best environment for a writer was. Had he asked the question back to her, she would surely have said that for an oral historian like her, it was a room full of voices—voices of otherwise forgotten chapters in American history, culture and society.

Above: Yeri wears a top by Hyejin Kim, a vest by Kanghyuk, a dress by Soyoung Park and a headpiece by Keewon Shin. Right: She wears a jacket by Post Archive Faction, a cropped jacket and trousers by Hyein Seo and shoes by Salomon. Previous: Vaker wears a shirt and jacket by Kanghyuk and a vest by Hyein Seo.

Hair: Gabe Shin, Makeup: Seongseok Oh.

暴

音

Yeri wears a jacket by Hyein Seo and a vest by Soyoung Park.

Left: Yeri wears a shirt and jacket by Kanghyuk. Above: She wears a top and trousers by Hyein Seo, shoes by Salomon and a backpack by Keewon Shin.

Above: Yeri wears a shirt and jacket by Kanghyuk. Right: Vaker wears a vest and trousers by Hyein Seo, a shirt and jacket by Kanghyuk and shoes by Yowe.

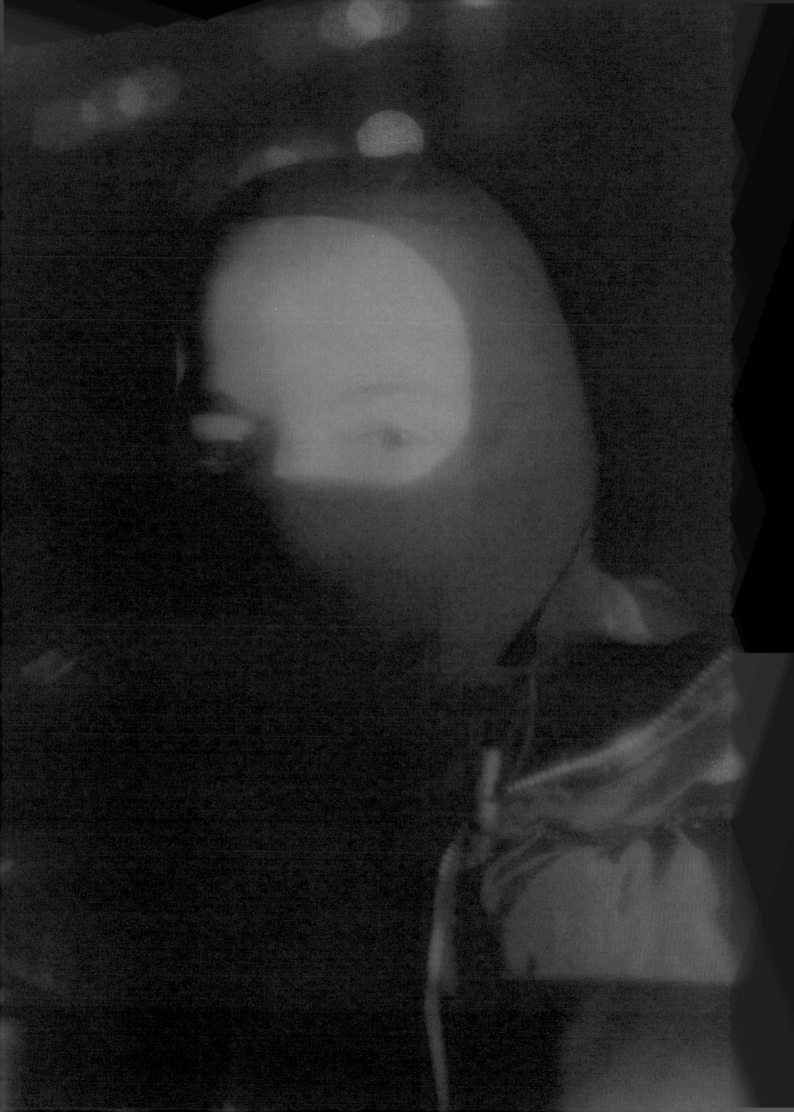

Above: Yeri wears a top and trousers by Hyein Seo, shoes by Salomon and a backpack by Keewon Shin.
Left: Vaker wears a jacket by Post Archive Faction, a vest by Hyejin Kim and a balaclava from the stylist's archive.

Above: Yeri wears a jacket by Post Archive Faction, a skirt by Hyein Seo and a top, vest, gloves, tights and shoes by Soyoung Park.
Left: Vaker wears a jacket by Hyein Seo and a turtleneck from the stylist's archive.

Above: Vaker wears a shirt and jacket by Kanghyuk. Right: He wears a jacket by Hyein Seo, trousers by Post Archive Faction and a turtleneck from the stylist's archive.

When Robert Mallet-Stevens insisted his architectural archive be destroyed on his death, much of his reputation vanished with it. Daphnée Denis pays a visit to the eponymous Parisian cul-de-sac where his legacy lives on. Photography by Romain Laprade

89

HÔTEL
MARTEL

Nestled in the 16th arrondissement of Paris, in an area known as the Village d'Auteuil near the city's western edge, rue Mallet-Stevens feels resolutely un-Parisian. Far from the French capital's traditional Haussmannian style, the modernist cul-de-sac, named after its architect, Robert Mallet-Stevens, once had critic Jean Gallotti ponder whether he may have been visiting another country. "The other day, in this lovely area of Auteuil, I thought I was transported to Morocco, in the new capital, where the chalk cubes of administrative palaces shine among pepper trees under the Mauritanian light," Gallotti wrote after the street's inauguration in the summer of 1927. Indeed, one can easily imagine how—with its unconventional mix of geometric shapes and white concrete walls pierced by large glass windows—the sunlit street could have evoked a more exotic location.

Today, the street exists as one of the few testaments to its namesake's vision. A contemporary of Le Corbusier whose penchant for aesthetics broke ranks with more rigorous forms of modernism, Mallet-Stevens demanded that his archive be destroyed upon his passing in 1945. His wish was granted, and, for decades, his work fell into oblivion—partly because his untimely death meant he could not participate in reconstruction efforts after World War II. It was only in the 1980s, when the street risked being torn down, that a collective of admirers lobbied to rehabilitate his legacy as an essential figure of France's modernism movement.

Most of the buildings on the lot, including the architect's own house and agency, have been altered to add more living space. The home of twin brothers Jan and Joël Martel, sculptors and close collaborators of Mallet-Stevens, stands as an untouched exception and the best-kept example of his approach to residential architecture and interior design. Built around a large cylindrical staircase linking a sculpture workshop to three private apartments (for the brothers and their father), Hôtel Martel juxtaposes square shapes and wide terraces covered in plants, as if they were bleachers. Per Mallet-Stevens' instructions, the abundant greenery was meant to "harmonize with the calm architectural lines," creating a garden-city of sorts in a street "exclusively devoted to rest," where all businesses would be banned. From the outside, the lower floor of the Martel house disguises the real dimensions of the studio: an impressive play with dislocated volumes creates a surprisingly vast space, where stairs lead down to a large area below ground level, while a mezzanine overlooks the room.

In 1927, Mallet-Stevens completed a summer residence in Hyères for art patrons Charles and Marie-Laure de Noailles. The villa inspired the surrealist artist Man Ray's 1929 film *Les Mystères du Château de Dé* and is today run as an arts center.

Mallet-Stevens was fascinated with Viennese Secessionist style and was heavily influenced by one the movement's founders, Austrian architect Josef Hoffmann.

"It's the archetypical Art Deco house with cubist influences," writes Éric Touchaleaume, an antiques dealer specializing in France's mid-20th-century design and architecture. He owns Jan Martel's apartment as well as the studio, now a showroom for his business, Galerie 54. Touchaleaume, who grew up in the area, says it was a childhood dream to live on rue Mallet-Stevens: "I used to love walking my dog in this peaceful alley, which seemed abandoned due to the lack of care for the buildings," he says. Later, after he started dealing antiques, he bought several sculptures from the Martel family, who remained in the brothers' house until the 1990s (he credits them with keeping the villa in its original state). One of those pieces, a plaster of the monumental religious sculpture *La Trinité*, greets Galerie 54 clients and visitors at the entrance of the studio.

It seems only appropriate that Touchaleaume, an antiques dealer trading in the likes of other modernists such as Le Corbusier and Charlotte Perriand, wound up setting up shop in Hôtel Martel. Both Le Corbusier and Perriand had been founding members of the Union des Artistes Modernes, a collective Mallet-Stevens spearheaded to break away from the more conservative Société des Artistes Décorateurs. Shocked by their peers' display of inaccessible luxury crafts at the 1925 Art Deco Exhibition in Paris, the group pledged to create avant-garde projects that would fulfill a more social role, putting functionality over ornament and promoting the use of industrial materials including glass, cement and metal.

Still, Mallet-Stevens, who grew up in a well-off family and exclusively worked for a rich clientele, was in turn criticized for his perceived elitism. As architectural historian Richard Becherer recounts, one of the most stinging attacks came after the inauguration of the Mallet-Stevens street, which was commissioned by a banker. "No building conceived with an emphasis on luxury and limitlessness can today maintain any meaning whatsoever in the history of architecture," Swiss critic Sigfried Giedion scathingly assessed in 1927.

The Martel brothers' house, however, proves the architect's approach was more functional than Giedion would give him credit for. The studio and apartments were designed with practicality in mind: large sliding doors allowed sculptures to be carried in and out of the workshop, and terrazzo floors were easily washed. "Hôtel Martel was designed for artists," Galerie 54's website says. "More precisely, for sculptors working with clay, plaster and stone. No doubt this is why its modernity is more radical, anticipating by half a century the minimalist industrial aesthetics of the loft."

That said, it is undeniable that Mallet-Stevens' focus on aesthetics could have irked some of his more austere contemporaries, as Becherer indicates. Heavily influenced by the Viennese Secession's all-encompassing view of the arts, which sought to integrate different fields like design and decoration, he thrived working across art forms. He was involved with the world of fashion, for instance, creating modernist shop fronts for brands including Bally shoes and Alfa Romeo, which clashed with their more traditional surroundings. And a firm believer that cinema was the only true modern artistic medium, he also designed film sets, most famously staging Marcel L'Herbier's silent picture *L'Inhumaine*, a tale of love lost between an actress and an engineer. His futuristic decors purported to be a visual cue of the characters' states of mind.

Mallet-Stevens' cinematic eye is apparent in one of Hôtel Martel's most striking features: the spiral staircase, which wraps around two mirrors fixed at the bottom and on the ceiling of the house, conveying an impression of infinity going up and down. The architect's philosophy of working hand-in-hand with trusted artists is equally on display, from the stainless steel door handles designed by avant-garde metal artisan Jean Prouvé, to the stained glass at the top of the stairs crafted by artist Louis Barillet. Touchaleaume, who like the Martel brothers lives above the studio, set out to bring Jan's apartment and the workshop back as close as possible to their original state, using original wall colors whenever possible. By trade, he says, antiques dealers like himself feel a duty to salvage heritage pieces, even before they are considered as such: "I always felt it was my mission, that's the beauty of my line of work."

Hôtel Martel entered France's list of historic monuments in 1975, more than three decades after Mallet-Stevens death, as efforts to unearth the architect's legacy started to pick up. While most passers-by may remain unfamiliar with his name, the Parisian alley, a microcosm of his approach to design, now attracts groups of aficionados looking to pay their respects to an essential figure of France's modernity.

"Hôtel Martel was designed for artists. More precisely, for sculptors."

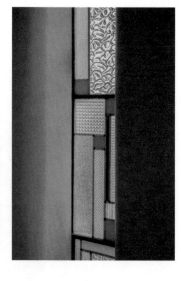

Mallet-Stevens was meticulous in his process and scrupulous with detail, coordinating a team of sculptors, glaziers, lighting designers and metalworkers on his projects.

When rue Mallet-Stevens was inaugurated in 1927, it was described admiringly in the press as a collection of "curious and luxurious buildings."

Essay:

Who's Laughing Now?

Words by Stephanie d'Arc Taylor

During the Trump presidency, late-night TV hosts made more jokes targeted at the White House than at any point in the genre's history. So why did so many liberal and politically engaged viewers choose to change the channel? Stephanie d'Arc Taylor charts the decline of the late-night comedy format and considers the alternatives.

Frequently, and for a variety of reasons, the year 2014 feels like several millennia ago. This sensation is particularly acute when watching old clips of *The Tonight Show* with Jimmy Fallon making jokes about President Barack Obama's love of golfing in his opening monologue. But even more uncanny is the idea that 11 million people tuned in to watch Fallon do the monologue live.

In 2019, an average of only two million people watched Fallon's opening monologue. Viewership for late-night comedy has plummeted across the board. According to a former Fallon producer speaking to the *Hollywood Reporter*, Fallon's steep decline—as well as the relative success of the more overtly political Stephen Colbert—may be attributed to viewers wanting a larger dose of politics with their comedy than ever before.

The glory days of late-night comedy, in which David Letterman, Jay Leno and other genial middle-aged white men would make gently ribald jokes to starlets smiling toothy smiles, seem as hazily remote as a Norman Rockwell Thanksgiving dinner. The world is more urgent now, says comedian Kate Willett, who co-hosts the leftist feminist comedy podcast *Reply Guys*, and people's dietary needs are different when it comes to media. "People in the US are following politics a lot more now," says Willett over Zoom from her apartment in Brooklyn. "So much wild stuff is happening that it's really noticeable to people."

Comedy writer David Litt agrees. In a former life, Litt wrote speeches for Barack Obama, including the president's memorable addresses to several assemblies of the White House Correspondents' Dinner. "You don't really get to be neutral in America today," says Litt, from his office in Washington, D.C. "Comedy has to figure out what to do about that. The comedians who have been the most successful are the ones who are recognizing that circumstances have really changed. It's like if your house caught fire and you just continued the conversation you were having before. That would be very off-putting."

Politics and comedy have always gone hand in hand. Jokes about politicians are evergreen fodder for dinner parties and stand-up shows alike. They work largely because they are universally relatable. "So much of comedy is about finding the absurd in our everyday lives," says Litt, "and few things are quite as absurd as politics."

Politicians being funny can also work, to diffuse tension or gauge a crowd. After his 1981 assassination attempt, Ronald Reagan cracked wise to his team of surgeons as he was being wheeled into the operating theater: "Please tell me you're all Republicans."[1] Humor can also get at an unacknowledged reality hovering in a room, says Litt. "If a politician tells a joke and everybody laughs, that shows that there's a kernel of truth there."

In fact, the first time any politician publicly mentioned the now gener-

1. During the Cold War, the CIA collected a secret cache of Soviet jokes. President Reagan reportedly found one joke so funny he started using it himself. It goes: "An American tells a Russian that the United States is so free that he can stand in front of the White House and yell, 'To hell with Ronald Reagan.' The Russian replies: 'This is nothing. I can stand in front of the Kremlin and yell, 'To hell with Ronald Reagan,' too.'"
—

2. In 2016, Trump jokes outnumbered those about Hillary Clinton by a factor of three. In 2020, Colbert and Fallon made Trump the target of 97% of their jokes about candidates.
—

ally acknowledged truth that the Republican party has a special relationship with Russian President Vladimir Putin was when Barack Obama joked about it at the 2014 White House Correspondents' Dinner. The joke didn't really land, though, until Obama started talking about conservative political commentator Sean Hannity's preoccupation with Putin's topless photos. "Now the fact that the right is in bed with Putin is common knowledge," says Litt, "and it's something Democrats talk about all the time."

Politics and comedy work so well together that recently a handful of actual comedians have been elected to high office all over the world. In 2019, Ukraine elected Volodymyr Zelensky, a former television star and professional comedian, as president. Guatemala, Slovenia, Italy and Iceland have also sent former satirists and comedians to their highest offices. Even Donald Trump was a comedian in his way—a fun-house amalgamate of a clown, an insult comic, and a physical satirist.

But just as there is more comedy in politics, plenty of us are finding politics less funny. Many point to Trump's election as accelerating the shift away from the broad, gentle late-night comedy of a bygone era (you know, the aughts). In the anxiety age of Trump's America, comedians no longer had the luxury of simply being funny for funny's sake. "The number of comedians stepping back and asking, 'What is the purpose of my comedy?' is higher than ever," says Litt. "The number of comedians saying, 'It's about making people laugh and that's all that matters' is lower."

But Trump's election coincided with (or was perhaps helped along by) an increasing fragmentation of the media landscape due to the internet and social media. To be successful either financially or in terms of reach, contemporary media personalities don't need a television studio or even hordes of listeners. Millions of people, literally, have bought mics and audio software off the internet and launched podcasts—as of 2020, there are over two million podcasts registered with Google.

Political podcasts have been part of this population explosion, on both sides of the political spectrum. They are frequently characterized by pundits making fun of people who don't agree with them. Media channels associated

"You don't really get to be neutral in America today. It's like if your house caught fire and you just continued the conversation you were having before."

with the self-described "dirtbag left," a term coined by one of the hosts of the podcast *Chapo Trap House*, combine comedy with condescension—and a fair amount of anger. Whereas traditional talk shows go for the low-hanging fruit that appeals to the largest possible audience, the internet, and podcasting in particular, has opened up a market for people with smaller followings. It's also created a way for these people to earn money. Patreon is a website that many left-leaning content creators use to sell subscriptions to their fans. In February 2020, *Chapo Trap House* became Patreon's highest-grossing account, earning over $160,000 per month.

Kate Willett's *Reply Guys* podcast is also listener-funded, but its hosts aren't pulling in that kind of money. At the end of 2020, according to their Patreon page, they had 118 subscribers paying a total of $586 per month. But, Willett says, there are perks to having a smaller following: "The only people we have to please are the people who like our show. It gives us the freedom to have stronger opinions."

The current stars of the late-night comedy circuit, says Willett, are largely carrying on the long-standing tradition of groveling for ratings—such as they are in 2020. "The late-night shows like *Stephen Colbert* are going to go for jokes that the most amount of people can relate to and not be offended by," she says. "They'll make fun of Trump for being orange or rude or dumb."[2]

On *Reply Guys*, Willett and her co-host don't have to pluck the low-hanging fruit. "We don't make fun of Trump for being orange," Willett says. "We take a broader look at what would make it possible to have a completely different country—not just getting Trump out of office."

But ironically, it was Willett's appearance on *The Late Show with Stephen Colbert* that gave her podcast a big boost in listeners—and not exactly those in their target market. "[Colbert] has a huge audience, and a lot of them are older people, what you might call boomers," she says. Not only are these listeners tuning in, but they're also responding to *Reply Guys'* left-leaning message. "We get these really cute messages from people who are in their 60s and 70s," she laughs. Even they, it appears, are open to learning a new trick or two. "It's so adorable to be a part of radicalizing boomers."

Drinking Wine With:
Grace Mahary

Kyla Marshell interviews the sommelier with a close to perfect palate—and a vision to change the industry.
Photography by *Valerie Chiang*

Location: Vinateria in Harlem, New York City

If things had gone a little differently, Grace Mahary might have been a WNBA star. As a teenager, the Edmonton, Canada, native had serious plans to pursue the sport as a teenager, determined as she was to see the world, any way she could. It might seem surprising that Mahary, an internationally recognized model with more than 200 runways under her belt, could have just as easily been a professional athlete. But Mahary herself has always known that she contains multitudes. A few years ago, she founded Project Tsehigh, a nonprofit which provides sustainable energy resources to communities in East Africa, including in her parents' native Eritrea. She followed that up by becoming co-owner of Los Angeles restaurant Chulita. Her latest pursuit is as a certified "somm," a credential she earned in 2019, but that has been years in the making. Speaking from her home in New York, Mahary explains that she has a few big goals for the wine industry beyond swishing and sipping.

KM: *What led you to become a sommelier?* **GM:** In early 2010, 2011, I started really getting into wine, and I got intimidated. As the years went on, I was like, "Why do I feel so intimidated by this world? If I'm in these luxurious spaces, why do I get looked at like I shouldn't be there?" I took the very clinical approach that I do with a lot of things and I just got really nerdy, started studying, went to school, and became certified. And now my hope is to amplify the voices of people that look like us, but also those who just typically don't have access to distributors, or restaurants, or customers that they'd love to have.

KM: *What does amplifying those voices look like?* **GM:** As simple as [pairing wine] with the foods that we grew up cooking. In Eritrea, we have a lot of spicy foods, and we eat injera, and there's no better pairing than our own fermented beverages—mes and suwa—which are like mead or honey wine, and beer. And finding fun, natural, organic and sustainable wines to pair with our foods has been really interesting for me. [It also means] highlighting the winemakers in Argentina that are women, or in South Africa that are Black women, or in California—and all across North America—that are minorities who don't normally get that experience. I also want to highlight sustainable, or as-natural-as-possible wines because at this point, if you're not trying to conserve the earth or at least lower your carbon footprint, then I don't know what planet you're living on.

KM: *In your forays into the wine world, what have you found to be the challenges for those marginalized groups?* **GM:** At every level of the industry, there are discrepancies for people of color. We don't own the land so we don't get to grow a lot of our stuff. Then there's distribution—once we get our wine out there, distributors aren't showcasing or including our product; retailers are not trying to sell it, or if they are, they limit the amount. And in service, it's like, "You should just have this because that's probably what you like," or "This is what you can afford." It's all in there, every level.

Blind taste tests are used as part of the sommelier exam to ensure that candidates can evaluate a wine without bias. By deploying knowledge of typical factors—such as grape varieties and the winemaking practices of different regions—a professional palate should be able to pinpoint a wine's origin with startling specificity.

"I've always felt that people are questioning my knowledge and my power in any industry that I walk into. It has been extremely frustrating."

KM: *What has your experience been, transitioning into this new career as an adult?* **GM:** I don't want to sound ungrateful, but I never wanted to model. I've always had other things going on. So modeling—I've treated it as a vehicle to do many things. This career has been about evolving as a model and creating art in a way that I found most interesting, but also to see what other doors could open. So I wouldn't use the word "transition" in this instance. I'm not a religious person—I'm more of a spiritual person, and I think transitioning is beautiful and I believe in karma and where we go in an afterlife. But I believe that in this life, I'm allowed to experience and indulge in as many things as I would like to without having to compromise my identity or [fit into] a label that society wants to use. I'm not only a model. I'm a certified somm, I am a nonprofit founder, and I am a daughter, sister, wife, person. I think I'll always be a model. Even when I'm a grandma, hopefully, but that doesn't mean that the other doors have to close in order for others to open.

KM: *I imagine that people might not necessarily take your passions outside of modeling seriously because they think of you as "just a pretty face." How do you deal with how people perceive you, and also carve out your own identity without always having to "prove" something?* **GM:** Thankfully, 15 years in modeling have helped me kind of deal with the fact that everyone is going to have their own perception of you and you can't control that. And the longer you try to control or manage that the more miserable you'll be. You learn pretty quickly as a model that you can't take things personally. It's about an image that people are creating. Unfortunately, along with creating that image comes ignorance—willful ignorance, and disrespectful treatment. But I will say that leaving home at 16 to model and work and go to school in Toronto, but then taking

the time until I was 20 or 21 to go worldwide, benefited my mental state and my courage to be able to enter the industry as such.

So yes, I've always felt that people are questioning my knowledge and my power in any industry that I walk into. It has been extremely frustrating. But I learned that the more I equip myself with knowledge, the more I'm ready to fix that. And it's almost like, Oh, I don't really care anymore, because the more prepared I am to go into these communities in East Africa and in America with solar energy programs, the less I care if anyone doesn't believe that I am capable of running a nonprofit. The more I provide the best wines for my friends and my family and the people around me, and they love them and they're excited and happy about them, and I'm happy about the wine that I'm selecting and learning about and winemakers that I'm meeting, the less I care that people don't think that I should be a somm, or can be a somm. So it's been very empowering to just rely on your knowledge and the hard work ethic that a lot of parents shove into you.

KM: *What would you say is at the core of all your various projects and interests?* **GM:** It's to even out the playing field. As the the daughter of immigrant parents who met on the war field, who had to work for every little thing that they have gotten, I understand what compromise looks like and what sacrifice looks like. And I also understand that it is important for humans to have that. To learn and to understand and to appreciate life. But there are ways to make things a little easier for others—just general things like groceries, income, electricity. Evening out the playing field for everyone is at the core of what I do. For people who look like us and for those who may never make more than $100,000 in their lives. And once we're there, I just want to be able to amplify and highlight everyone's voices in that space.

3.

Youth

114—176

ELISE BY OLSEN:

I HAD THAT AMBITION. *I WANTED* THAT AUDIENCE.

What does the world's youngest editor-in-chief do when they turn 21? Tom *Faber* interviews *Elise By Olsen*—the publishing maven who's forcing the fashion industry to actually listen to the young people it fetishizes. Photography by *Lasse Fløde* & Styling by *Afaf Ali*

"I feel like I don't really have a relationship to my age," Elise By Olsen tells me over Zoom from her bedroom in Oslo, Norway. "I just had my 21st birthday two weeks ago, and I was thinking about how my age has been taken away from me. The press always focused on the whole 'youngest editor' thing. It's a box the media has put me in since day one."

It's understandable why the media might focus on the "whole youngest editor thing" when writing about Olsen. At the age of 13, she launched a youth culture magazine, *Recens*, making her the world's youngest editor-in-chief (she couldn't claim the Guinness World Record, ironically, because she was too young for their age restrictions). Eight years later, the Norwegian is the very model of a precocious Gen-Z multi-hyphenate, with two magazines under her belt, consulting work at a dream list of fashion companies and the recent establishment of an international fashion library in Norway.

Given these achievements, I had expected that speaking to Olsen would be a serious affair, yet in conversation she proves quick and chatty, able to turn on a dime from full-on discourse mode to wry humor. After five years of traveling the world for work, she is grounded—back in her childhood bedroom in the basement of her parents' house. Her homecoming wasn't due to COVID-19, but because her father fell seriously ill two months before the pandemic. "I went home and felt I needed to stay around for his recovery," she explains. "I had just started to feel so un-present in everything that has to do with my life."

So in January 2020, Olsen decided she would spend the year at home. She gives me a webcam tour, pushing back ice-blonde hair—dyed the same spectral shade as her eyebrows— and revealing subtle black tattoos on each wrist. There is a desk, underneath a striking photo of an androgynous youth with a huge mane of curly ginger hair, taken by Norwegian photographer Torbjørn Rødland. On the other side of a dividing wall is a cozier sleeping space, where big fashion books and magazines with colorful spines are arranged on a wireframe shelf "for private research." Opposite, a bed is tucked snugly between the walls, overlooked by a large television which protrudes on a metal arm. She looks at it and giggles. "It's such a bachelor pad thing to have," she says.

Above: By Olsen wears a suit by Acne Studios and shoes by Bottega Veneta. Left: She wears a dress by Balenciaga. Previous: She wears a vintage hat and skirt.

*"In fashion, people hold onto their positions for way longer than is needed...
Just knowing when to stop is important."*

Olsen was born in this eastern Oslo suburb in 1999, and started her first blog at the age of eight—largely an outlet for concerns about homework and family dinners. In 2012, she and a group of friends launched Archetype, a popular Scandinavian blogging network for teens, splitting the cost of website upkeep between themselves. This inspired *Recens*, the youth culture magazine she founded at 13. Its first issue was a bit of a mess. "We put it together on a Word document," she says. "The images were super pixelated, the paper felt weird and there were grammar mistakes. But I wanted it to be in English, an international magazine, because I had that ambition. I wanted that audience."

Recens aimed to center the creative narratives of young people by allowing them to tell their own stories. It sat strangely in the fashion industry, which is obsessed with youth—but to look at, rather than to listen to. Olsen was not the only young person challenging fashion orthodoxy at the time; over in the US, a teenage Tavi Gevinson was gaining popularity for her fashion blog, *Style Rookie*. But unlike Gevinson, Olsen focused on print media. After the first issue of *Recens*, which she funded using her own money, she started to attract advertisers and began collaborating with her business partner and art director, Morteza Vaseghi, then twice her age. He helped transform the magazine into a glossy, professional publication which pointedly ignored the prevailing trends of Scandinavian minimalism, matte paper and monochrome fashion spreads.

Her parents, who worked in customs and logistics, were unperturbed by their 13-year-old daughter going straight from school to an office to work on her magazine. They thought it was just a phase—but it never passed. *Recens* took off and Olsen dropped out of high school at 16 to work full-time. Working so young, she encountered a lot of preconceptions about her parents. "People believe I come from a cultural family or that my parents have been pushing me," she says, "but there was none of that. It's been very organic, and if I wanted to stop doing this today, they'd support me."

Over seven issues, *Recens* featured contributions from more than 500 people around the world, most of them under 25. It was a hit. And yet, just before her 18th birthday, Olsen decided to resign on principle: She considered it inauthentic to edit a youth magazine as an adult. By then Olsen was already considered a spokesperson for her generation—a TEDx talk she gave in 2016 is titled "A Manifest from Generation Z." While she now feels uncomfortable speaking for anything beyond her own experience, Olsen was at the vanguard of a social shift over the past decade which has seen younger people's voices being taken more seriously.

One of the striking anachronisms of *Recens* is that it was a print-only publication helmed by a digital native. Olsen has loved print since she was eight years old, when she used her pocket money to buy copies of *Dazed* and *Vogue Italia* from newsstands. "Back then, print felt like an antidote to the digital mindset I had," she explains. "It was the sensory connection, the smell and touch of it. I also liked the different pace—sitting down and giving all my attention to one object, not being stimulated by a bunch of different things like when you consume information online."

Olsen channeled this love into her second publication, *Wallet*, which she launched at 18. *Wallet* is more intellectual than *Recens*, and its form is just as provocative as its content. She analyzed declining print sales and decided big magazines were inconvenient, so she made Wallet an "anti-coffee table book"—slim enough to fit into a jeans pocket. Its ads are on perforated pages that can be torn out and there are blank pages at the back for note-taking. All of this encourages readers to interact with *Wallet*, to revel in its physicality and make it their own.

Wallet's manifesto is to "redeem fashion journalism," a barbed response to magazines devoid of cultural and institutional critique, where independent thought comes second to advertisements and branded content. "Fashion is traditionally looked on as a feminine field. It's something rich husband's wives play with on the side, not deemed worthy of critique like film or art," Olsen says. *Wallet* addresses the conversations that the fashion world isn't having: "It's about understanding the operations around fashion: the politics, the money, and the power."

Wallet has become essential reading for people seeking a critical lens on the industry, yet Olsen is planning to wrap it up after the 10th issue. This marks a trend in her professional life—perhaps, like her parents first suspected, each of these projects is just a phase before she moves on to something else. She offers a different explanation: "It feels like in fashion, people hold onto their positions for way longer than is needed. Look at Anna Wintour at *Vogue*. She is, in my opinion, completely irrelevant, steering the publication in a way which is fatal. Just knowing when to stop is important." Here, too, Olsen is riding the first wave of a societal shift: toward a 21st-century globalized industry of freelance creatives, digital nomads with shapeshifting careers who embrace their freedom, but perhaps worry about the absence of the professional security that their parents took for granted.

> *"If I could give advice to myself back then, I'd say to go even harder. You have nothing to lose."*

Publishing three issues of *Wallet* per year has not stopped Olsen from taking on a dizzying array of other jobs: curating art exhibitions, producing films, giving talks which are so popular that one about rethinking publishing was printed in book form last year. In 2018, she bought and renovated a 2,000-square-foot warehouse on a vineyard outside of Lisbon, Portugal, turning it into a studio-cum-living space, an experiment to see what she could get for the same amount of money as a tiny space in New York or London.

After this half-decade of "accelerated living," returning to roost in Oslo was a tough transition. "I felt like I was in lockdown from the moment my father got sick," she says. "It's been kind of lonely since my friends are spread out around the world, but actually it's been good for me. I spent these months confronting my feelings and I felt very balanced. There's a lot of nature near where I live. Oslo is like that, you can take the metro five minutes away and you're in the woods." Regular walks were an important part of her father's recovery, but Olsen also found them grounding. "I process a lot when I walk," she says. "It's like therapy."

She has used this time and focus to zone in on a new project—helming the launch of the International Library of Fashion Research in Oslo. It is pitched as a repository for fashion's printed material which includes, alongside books and magazines, commercial publications usually ignored by libraries such as lookbooks, catalogs and advertising posters. "I think that side of fashion is important to embrace because it's such an inherent part of the industry," Olsen says. "The creativity is very dependent on the commercial side."

The seed collection was donated by cultural critic and New York scenester Steven Mark Klein, one of several older figures who Olsen counts as a mentor. He packed up the publications, which filled a whole shipping container, and sent them by boat to Oslo, where the library has been offered a home by Norway's National Museum of Art, Architecture and Design. The library's digital incarnation opened in October 2020 with more than 5,000 publications available, though you cannot read them page-by-page, due to complications around publishing rights. The physical library is set to open in the spring, overseen by a board Olsen assembled including luminaries from Comme des Garçons, Prada and *i-D* Magazine.

Whether she's saving fashion's printed material or fighting to revolutionize its journalism, Olsen presents these missions in the language of responsibility. Plenty of teenagers feel frustrated by the cultural landscape, but few decide that it's their job to change things. Why, I ask, does it feel so personal to her? "It's a frustration I'm trying to grapple with, like creating the fashion library I wish had existed when I was younger," she says. "I have responsibilities toward my team, my readers, and especially the younger people who come along with me for the ride."

"It's a lot to take on," I say. "It's a lot to take on, indeed it is," she says, before smiling nervously and gazing out of her small bedroom window at the gray Norwegian sky. She looks like she's about to say something, and then thinks better of it. "It is, yep."

I ask how she reflects on her behavior as an editor-in-chief at 13, looking back. She thinks for a moment. "I had this naivety that young people have. It's good that I didn't know the reality of the fashion industry and the world at that age, because I would have become so cynical. But if I could give advice to myself back then, I'd say to go even harder. You have nothing to lose. Now I'm 21 and I can't hide behind my youth anymore. Back then it was the only thing to do—get up and out."

Though Olsen says she feels like her age has been taken away from her, it seems to me that she has always been totally in control. She used her youth while it was useful, and now that she has grown up and is taken more seriously, she has shrugged it off as easily as a winter coat.

In 2018, Gucci sponsored a short film about Olsen entitled *Youth Mode*, chronicling her work with *Recens* and her decision to resign at 18. In it we see an Olsen not often depicted in the media: laughing hysterically, dancing in a club, sitting in a bathtub and joking with friends. Being a normal teenager. I ask if she deliberately cultivates such a serious image in the press. She shrugs. "I feel like that's a very personal side that I don't feel the need to share."

The film ends with a teasing moment where an unidentified voice over the phone asks: "Do you ever feel like you missed out on anything, finding success so young?" The phone hangs up and the question goes unanswered as the credits roll. I bring this moment up with Olsen.

"You didn't answer that question in the film," I say. "Will you answer it now?"

She smiles. "It's a question I hear a lot from my family, friends and people in the industry: 'Do you feel like you've grown up too fast, or missed out on your youth, or whatever?' Honestly, I don't know the alternative. I feel like I've had a great childhood and teenage years. I've seen parts of the world at a very young age, met amazing people and had incredible conversations. That's fun to me." She looks out the window again. "I've chosen it, you know? And if I wanted something else, I would have chosen otherwise."

By Olsen wears a dress by Balenciaga.

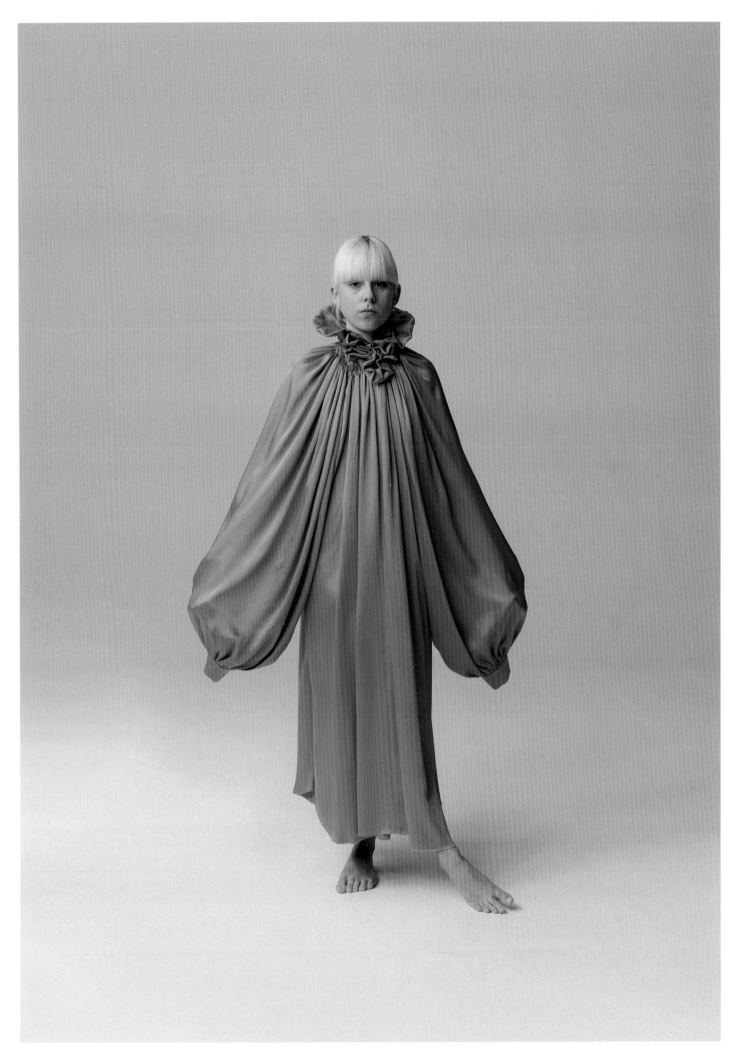

in a room and world of one's own. Photography by Romain Laprade & Styling by Camille Josephine Teisseire

Above: Thomas wears a cashmere polo top by Lanvin. Previous: He wears a tank top by BLUEMARBLE and a ring by Tant d'Avenir.

Hair: Taan Doan, Makeup: Helena Henrion, Set Design: David de Quevedo

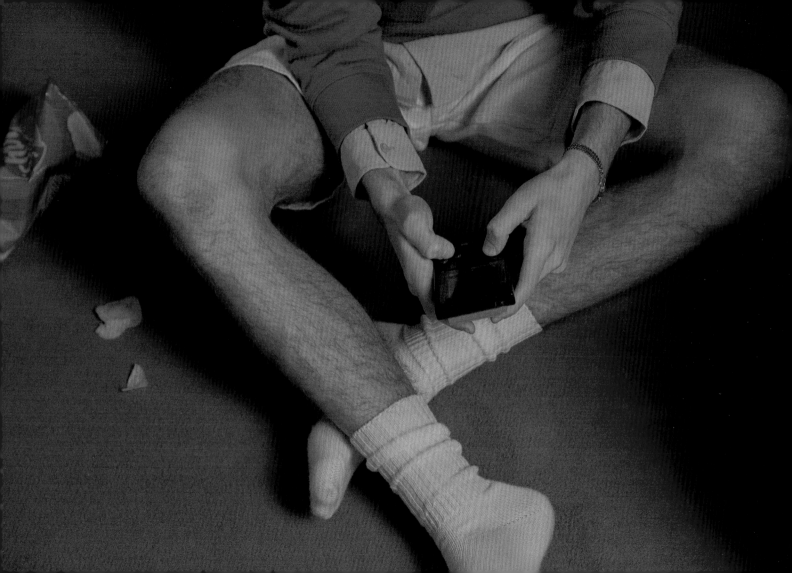

THE NEXT
BEST THING

132

From Tamagotchis to cassette tapes: A celebration of the tech that shaped a generation. Photography by *Yana Sheptovetskaya*

THE TAMAGOTCHI

For many millennials, their first pet was small, demanding and chronically incontinent. When Japanese company Bandai launched the Tamagotchi in 1997, preteens around the world were enamored with the virtual creature that required its owner to feed it, discipline it and clean up its messes. This gameplay proved so addictive that *The Baltimore Sun* labeled those in its grips "the Tamagotchi generation." Schools banned them and parents complained that they were forced to babysit them. "It's the most powerful product I've ever heard of, in terms of what it demands from a child," one psychologist remarked to *The New York Times*.

THE CD

In 1982, a German factory manufactured an unassuming piece of polycarbonate plastic. The slender, laser-encoded compact disc represented a years-long collaboration between Philips and Sony to develop a superior alternative to the LP record. The result was lightweight, resilient and could be mass-produced. Several years later, Sony released a portable CD player that allowed consumers to carry their music around with them. By the time the CD celebrated its 25th anniversary, its success could be measured by its ubiquity: 200 billion had been sold.

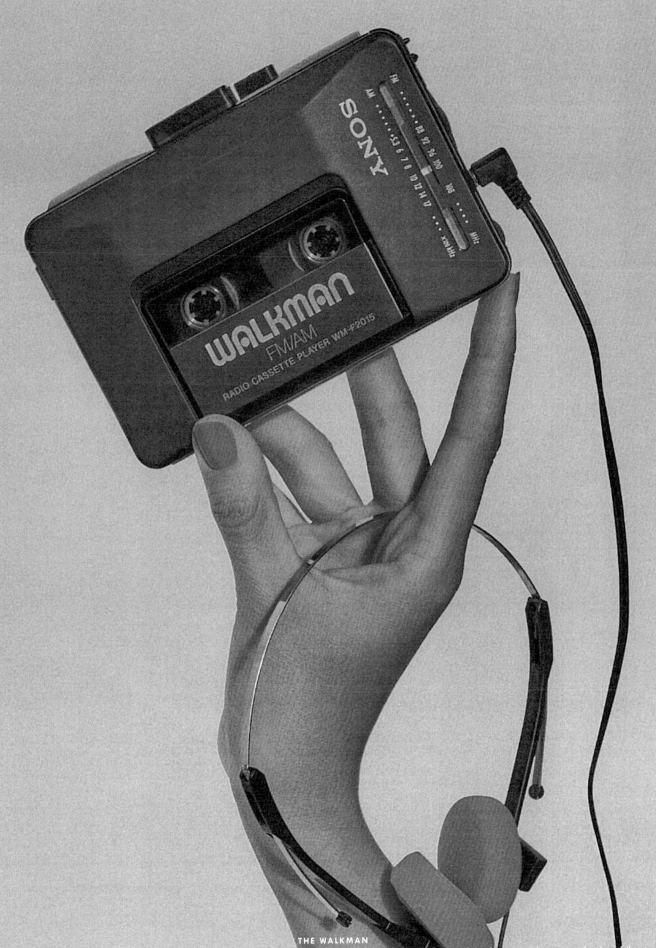

THE WALKMAN

Sony co-founder Masaru Ibuka enjoyed listening to opera when he traveled for business. The only problem, as he complained to an employee, was the size of the stereo tape recorder he carried with him. In 1979, a pioneering solution was designed: a handheld, battery-operated cassette player with headphones that was dubbed the "Walkman." Its success was immediate. As the first portable device, the Walkman revolutionized people's ability to enjoy music on the go. And go they did—according to *Time*, at the height of the Walkman's popularity, when it was used as a companion to workouts, the number of people who walked for exercise increased by 30%.

THE MOTOROLA RAZR V3

Described by *Men's Health* as a "gleaming, anodized-aluminum, look-at-me package," the Motorola Razr V3 was 2004's hottest accessory. Until its arrival, mobile phones had been chunky blocks of plastic produced with functionality in mind. But the futuristic V3—with its super-slim flip frame and glowing blue backlight—proved the power of design-led technology. First revealed to a select crowd of fashion journalists in Copenhagen, the Razr quickly became a status symbol. Its star quality was cemented with a wildly expensive model by Dolce & Gabbana, plated in liquid gold.

THE GAMEBOY COLOR

"The main new feature of the Gameboy Color is the terrific reflective color LCD display," raved a self-professed "video game freak" on her gadgets blog in 1998. It had been nine years since Nintendo released their first handheld console, an ungainly-looking box whose screen displayed games in varying shades of gray. This new iteration, in comparison, boasted sophisticated technology that saw its screen support a 56-color palette that felt far more animated. The Gameboy Color's arrival roughly coincided with another seminal Nintendo invention: the Pokémon video game series. Together, they would dominate the lives of gamers until the Gameboy Color was discontinued in 2003.

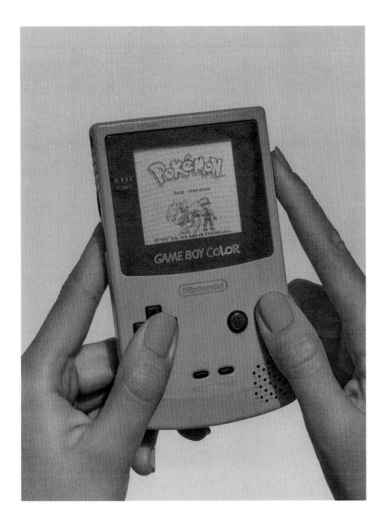

THE CASSETTE

Mass-produced cassette tapes were first introduced in 1964. Small and portable, the tape's initial appeal lay in its convenience. But by the '80s, cassette sound quality had improved enough for Maxell, a leading manufacturer, to produce an advertisement that boasted of its "high fidelity" audio. In it, a man slouched coolly in a designer armchair that faced a speaker. After a white-gloved butler inserted a cassette tape, Wagner's "Ride of the Valkyries" began to play—and the sheer force of the sound waves blew the man's martini glass backward into his outstretched hand.

AWK—

When you really can't style it out. Photography by *Ted Belton* & Styling by *Nadia Pizzimenti*

WARD

SNAP (previous): Whak wears a sweater by Nouveau Riche and trousers by Junya Wantanabe.
Mo wears a sweater by Nouveau Riche, trousers by JW Anderson. Both wear belts from the stylist's personal archive.

SHE'S BEHIND YOU: AJ wears a blazer and shorts from Hugo by Hugo Boss, a T-shirt by Acne Studios and socks by Uniqlo.
Effy wears a coat by Issey Miyake, tights by Simons and shoes by Prada.

Hair & Makeup: Ronnie Tremblay. Casting: Marc Ranger

SPINACH SMILE: Fiona wears a sweater and dress by Hermès.

HAT HAIR: AJ wears a jacket and hat by Latre and a shirt by Marni.

LEFT HANGING: Whak wears a jumpsuit by Nouveau Riche. Effy wears a dress by Markoo.

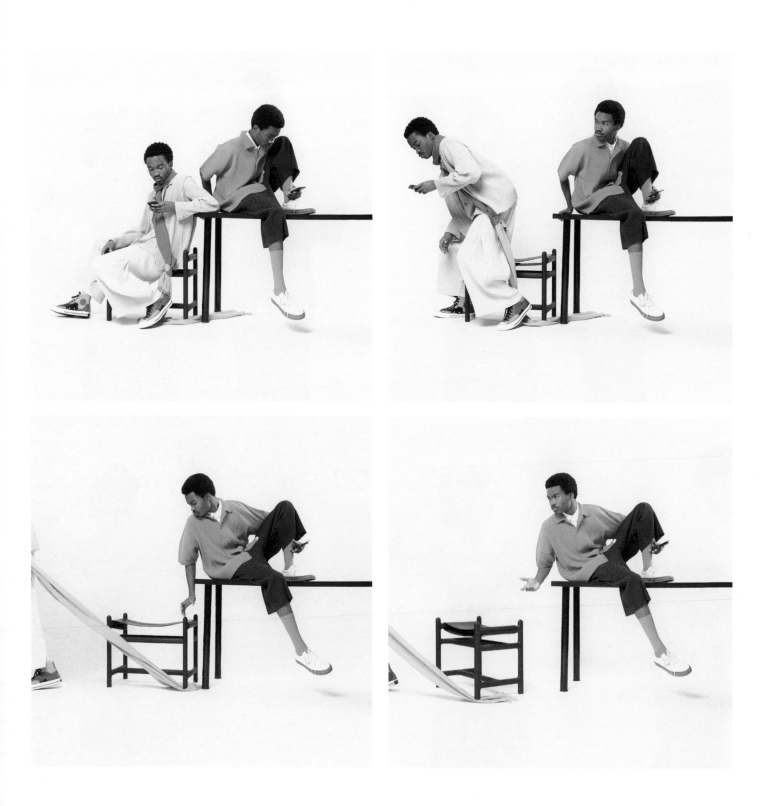

NOT SO FAST: Whak wears a shirt, jacket and trousers by Homme Plissé Issey Miyake, scarves by Simons and shoes by Converse.
Mo wears a shirt by COS, a jacket and trousers by Homme Plissé Issey Miyake, socks by Simons and shoes by Vans.

UNLUCKY TUCK: Fiona wears a blouse and skirt by Boutet, tights by Simons and shoes by Salvatore Ferragamo.
Mo wears a turtleneck by Andrew Coimbra, trousers by Boss, a jacket by Kenzo, socks by Uniqlo and shoes by Adidas.

How can a young adult fiction author tackle racism, inequality and incarceration—but not rob teen readers of their optimism? *Okechukwu Nzelu* interviews *Nic Stone*. Photography by *Corey Woosley*

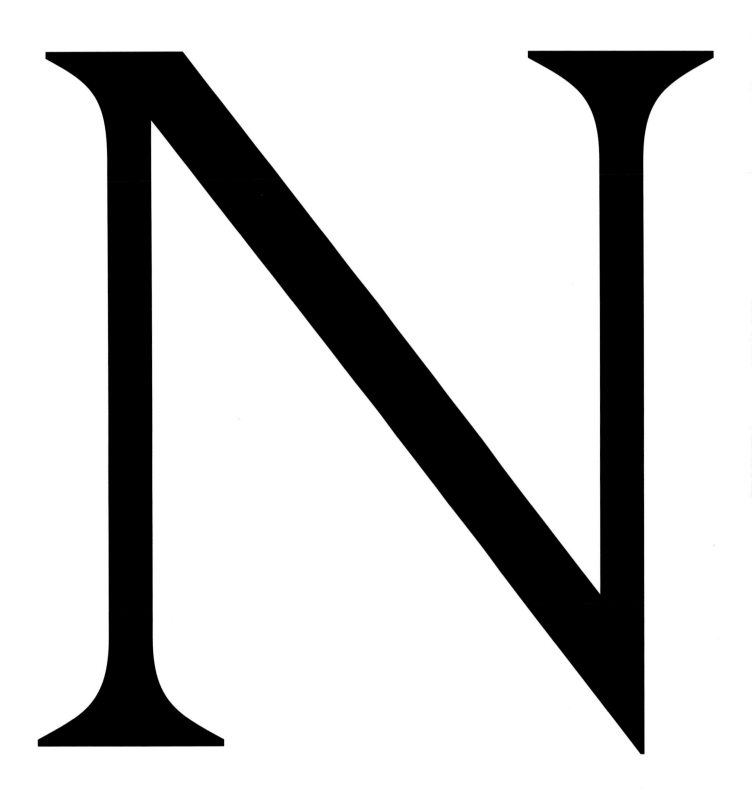

Nic Stone's young adult novels tackle some of the most difficult subject matters imaginable. Her bestselling 2017 novel, *Dear Martin*, tells the story of a young Black man coming to grips with the work and philosophy of Martin Luther King Jr., while experiencing police brutality in today's America. The sequel, her latest book, *Dear Justyce*, was inspired by two of Stone's teenage mentees, who asked her to write a book that represented them. Stone's writing succeeds because of her

strength of heart: One of the things that makes her books (and our conversation) so memorable is her remarkable generosity of spirit. She describes herself as an "eternal optimist," but Stone also has a keen understanding of human nature and of history. Black, queer and a mother herself, she is under no illusions about the injustices faced by marginalized young people and her writing is both empathetic and bracingly honest.

When I speak to Stone, she's at home in Atlanta and America's presidential election hangs in the balance. I have been obsessively refreshing news websites, but the author has wisely stayed away from them—waiting for a solid outcome to emerge, and preserving her peace in the meantime. Somehow, amid so much uncertainty, Stone provides a serenity that tides me over during the uncertain days of vote counting that follow.

ON: *Your writing is inspiring, but it also tells difficult truths about the world. Was that hard for you to do, as a writer for young people?* **NS:** Honestly, no; it just felt vital. It's important that I know what people might be thinking when I step into a room. My sons need to know that when they step into a room, people might assume that they're dangerous. However, the flip side of that is, with that knowledge of what other people might be thinking, there needs to be a knowledge of who you are and what you're capable of. So, with all my work, my goals will always be both enlightenment and empowerment. I want my readers to know what's out there, but I also want them to know that they get to decide how they are going to move to the world and what they believe about themselves. In the introduction to James Baldwin's *The Fire Next Time*, there's this part where he's writing this letter to his nephew. And he says something like: *Yes, people might call you the N-word—but is that what you are?* I want to make sure that kids understand that the only person who has authority over your identity is you. You have to decide what you believe about yourself.

ON: *When you were young, was writing a career you imagined for yourself?* **NS:** I was 27 when I started writing. It's not that I didn't want to write before, but when I hit middle school, all of the things that we were told we had to read to prove that we were literate either didn't have me in them, or they had people who looked like me in them living lives that I certainly did not want to emulate. So, for a while, I felt like I didn't have the imagination to tell stories. In college, I got very into Toni Morrison, Alice Walker, Zora Neale Hurston, Ralph Ellison, Richard Wright and Ernest Gaines. But in high school, it was all Twain and Shakespeare and all of these dead white dudes, and they just didn't help me set some kind of standard. So it took me a while to even realize I could be a storyteller. I'm glad that it happened how it did, because it's nice to realize you're wrong about yourself in that way. And there's no stopping now.

> *"I want to make sure that kids understand that the only person who has authority over your identity is you."*

"Young adult fiction" is a term used to describe books with an intended audience aged 12 to 18. However, estimates suggest that more than 50% of the genre's readers are adults.

Dear Martin was written in the form of letters to Martin Luther King Jr. Stone wanted to explore how his teachings would translate to the Black Lives Matter movement.

ON: *Your work is now taught in schools. What does that feel like?* **NS:** I'm still in shock. The number of text messages and DMs on Instagram I get from kids is so wild.

ON: *Do you worry that your books might be misinterpreted by teachers unfamiliar with the sorts of stories you're telling?* **NS:** Of course there are going to be hiccups anytime you are making a vast and sweeping change to what is taught in a classroom. There's a learning curve, and I'm not mad about it. In order to teach something new, you have to learn something new. I get the privilege of interacting with a lot of teachers and there's definitely a willingness to be wrong about stuff, which is really important when you're interacting with young people.

ON: Dear Martin *starts with a young man trying to understand the teachings of Martin Luther King and apply them to the world today. Do you feel that the messages of history's heroes need to be reinterpreted, to reach young people today?* **NS:** Absolutely. And I say that as a young person who didn't get the full story. I remember my US history class in 2001: Our textbook had a paragraph on the slave trade, and half a page on the civil rights movement. The slave trade lasted more than 200 years, and there was a paragraph! When it comes to historical figures like Dr. King, I didn't really learn the whole truth about him until I started researching for myself. I think that we do kids—especially marginalized kids—a disservice when we don't tell them the whole truth about the people who have made it possible for them to even be where they are. And I just get sick and tired of hearing people quote Dr. King, not only in opposition to things he would have supported, but in support of things he would have opposed.

On MLK Day this year, the vice president [Mike Pence] quoted Dr. King, during an address he was giving about the need for a border wall! And I was furious, because people aren't learning about Dr. King, and the fullness of his philosophies, teachings and principles. So, I will continue to address these historical figures in my work, because I do want young people to be interested in them, but I also want young people to learn about them accurately. Don't come at me with, *Dr. King was peaceful.* He was not peaceful, he was non-violent. Those are not the same thing.

ON: *What messages do you want young people to take from your writing?* **NS:** I think the message of Dear Justyce is something to the effect of, *Everybody is deserving of somebody who believes in them.* And a lot of the weight of *Dear Justyce* actually exists in the author's note: If you have had people believe in you, pay it forward. If you have never had anybody believe in you, know that I believe in you. Another thing I really want young people to get from *Dear Justyce* is the fact that compassion and empathy are choices that you have to make; they don't come naturally. Most of us are so focused on our own survival that we don't necessarily take the time to empathize. So, I want young people to choose compassion, and to recognize that they don't need permission to be compassionate; they don't need permission to empathize. You can decide to empathize with another person, and to believe in the people around you, and to honor their humanity.

"If you have had people believe in you, pay it forward."

In a 2019 interview with *Publishers Weekly*, Stone said she had been surprised by the success of *Dear Martin* just eight months after Angie Thomas' *The Hate U Give*, which also tackled the racial profiling of young people. "It seemed at the time there could only be one of each thing," she said. "The industry is changing."

N O S E

What advice would you give your younger self?
An artist, a writer, a conductor, a curator, a rabbi and a robot pen missives to the past.
Photography by *Christian Møller Andersen*

TELE TOTE

Dear pre-teen Abby/YA:

I know, you feel alone. You are a girl the world isn't listening to. They claim you are a boy.

You Should know:

· You are not alone - there are millions like you!!

· You CAN do it. You will survi-ve, and a fun, successfull life is waiting for you. Live on,

PS:
Pay more attention to Mommy's cooking...

Rock on,
with Love.
Abby C. Stein - 2020

Rabbi Abby Stein is the first publicly transgender woman to have grown
up in the ultra-Orthodox Hasidic Jewish community. She was interviewed in Issue Thirty-Eight, the Rituals Issue.

Dear Michael,

Always be true to yourself
and trust your instincts.
Your dreams will come true,
just don't give up!

Hang in there!!!

XO
MB

Michael Bargo is a design dealer and interior designer in New York. He was interviewed for the Last Night column in Issue Thirty-Eight.

Hey Michel,

Your here out of the future. (took some trouble to get here...) Important: I did not let you down regarding dreams and aspirations!
Cheers to that!!! :)

Wish we could hang out to-gether, would be fun a hilarious with this age difference! But hey, now may we do!
Miss you!

Yours,

Yan.

Michaël Borremans is a Belgian painter represented by David Zwirner. He was interviewed at his studio in Issue Thirty-Three.

Dear André,

I remember so well the day you turned seventeen. I remember your insecurities, your dreams, your loves, your resentments and regrets, your thirst for so many things, some undefined, others still unknown, maybe unreal. I remember them because I've never outgrown them — and hope I never do. I know you're coddling many hopes, and I know you've taught yourself not to trust them, because you've known failure and fear it no less than you fear success. Here is my advice: learn to trust what's in your heart now, even if it seems a whim, and don't let it die or be dulled away by what we call wisdom and experience. Don't waste your time, as I did, pursuing what others taught me to seek. Seek instead what, despite risks and challenges, thrills you and makes you happy. Don't fight it. You may adapt but you won't change. Stay who you are!

Yours,
The older you, André

André Aciman is the author of more than a dozen works of fiction and non-fiction, including the novel *Call Me By Your Name*. He was interviewed in Issue Twenty-Nine.

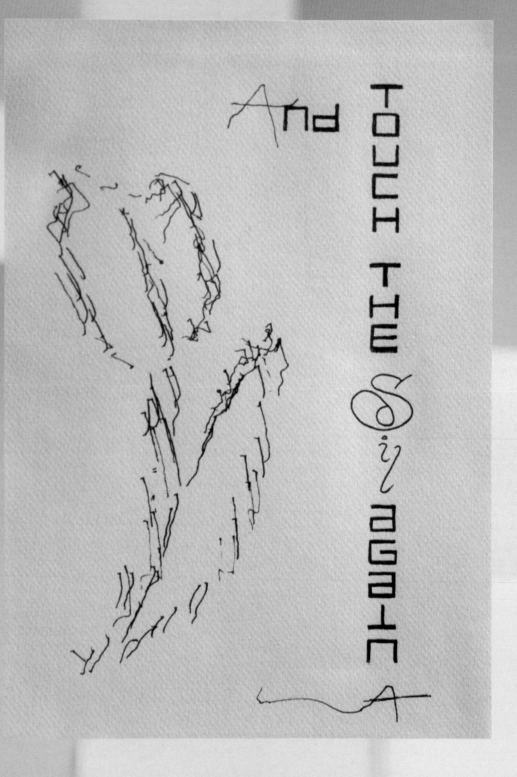

And TOUCH THE Sky again

Ai-Da is a robot. She was profiled in Issue Thirty-Five, the Change Issue. This AI-generated message
reflects her environmental concerns. "She speaks both to her younger self, and to a younger humanity," a representative explains.

Dear Roderick,

A couple of tips to help you along the way...

1. Depth to your work comes from Experience and hard work.

2. There is no substitute or short cuts to preparation.

3. You ~~will~~ must become your most important teacher

4. A Healthy self-confidence must be...
   - nurtured
   - protected
   - evaluated

5. Examine what you don't know and fill in the gaps.

6. Reflect! then move on.

7. As a musician, Always Sing! Never hold back! Leave everything on stage!

8. Don't tear someone down to build yourself up.

9. Always be grateful

10. Opportunities may not always come when you expect them to, but be ready when they do!

All the best to you!
Roderick

Roderick Cox is a Berlin-based American conductor and winner of The Sir Georg Solti Conductor award. He was interviewed in Issue Thirty-Six.

Essay:

Parental Control

Words by Tom Faber

Parents of older children often fret over how to regulate their online presence. But for the vast majority of millennial offspring, social media begins much earlier, with images and anecdotes shared on their parents' account. With a new generation of teenagers now discovering the digital footprint created for them, Tom Faber *considers the dos and don'ts of "sharenting."*

Place your hand in front of a child's eyes, and everything disappears. Take it away again—peekaboo!—and the world rushes back into existence like a wave filling a rock pool. This simple game has much to tell us about infant development. It underlines the omnipotence of the parent, who can dramatically shift their child's horizons on a whim. It emphasizes, too, the slow dawning of self-awareness in children; they are six months old before they learn their bodies are separate from their mother, three years old before they recognize themselves in a mirror, and five by the time they understand they are fixed, perceivable selves—beings bounded by flesh and skin.

For centuries, this was the final stage of self-awareness, but today, for the first generation who are younger than Instagram, younger even than TikTok, there is a new final step: the first time the child Googles themselves, realizing they exist in a virtual public domain where their image is infinitely reproducible, shareable and indelible.

This epiphany of digital consciousness is now commonplace: Over 90% of American children have photos posted on parents' social media by the age of two, with 23% making their internet debut pre-birth as a blob on a sonogram scan.[1] Children's reactions to first encountering their digital footprint vary wildly; some are horrified, others embarrassed, or even excited. Internet crusaders rail against the phenomenon of "sharenting"—parents feverishly uploading every walk in the park and mushy mealtime. They say this behavior infringes on the safety and privacy of our children and even hinders their development. This is terra incognita for the first generation of parents rooted in social media, and poses many tricky questions and uncharted terrain for today's children, the first to grow up and realize that their whole life story to date has already been written for the public by someone else.

Latham Thomas runs Mama Glow, a maternity lifestyle brand, and has 130,000 followers on Instagram. She describes social media as "a powerful tool, but a cruel master": It drives her business, but she reminds herself to be intentional about how she posts. She has shared images of her son, Fulano, since he was 10, and created an independent profile for him after he first received press attention as a child DJ. Since he was already in the public eye, she didn't see her posts as a problem.

Fulano, now 17, reflects on those early photos. "I had about a thousand followers and I was like—Oh, this is really cool. I thought I was a celebrity." He and his mother have since shared management of his public account without much trouble. When Thomas posted a photo of her son sleeping, which he viewed as "a violation," she promised not to do that again (though, he notes, she never took that particular post down). These days he leaves his public account mostly to his mom, "because I don't remember to post much," and instead uses his private account, just for friends, which is primarily used for messaging and browsing memes. His digital presence is divided into the professional narrative, mostly curated by his mother, and his private, personal outlet.

Not everyone can claim, like Thomas, thousands of followers and pictures at the pool with Gwyneth Paltrow, but regular parents can also benefit from sharing their family life online. It can help stay connected to geographically dispersed friends and relatives, not unlike a round-robin letter sent at Christmas. Having a child can be an isolating time, as new parents find themselves suddenly stuck at home, removed from their usual social circles, and the internet provides a way to connect. Those whose children suffer from health problems can find valuable support communities online.

Inevitably, every internet trend attracts its haters. The blog *STFU, Parents* was founded in 2009 to lampoon sharenting on social media, satirizing "the jaw-dropping, self-indulgent, and occasionally rage-inducing world of parental overshare." It appealed to the venerable human tradition of judging others' parenting: There's nothing some people love more than to tut and murmur, "I would never do that to my children." Leah Plunkett, a law professor and author of the book *Sharenthood*, remarks that while some parents do cross the line, such critiques also stem from a deep-rooted social judgment of mothers. "Throughout the generations, moms have been frequently targeted in public discourse," she says, "from what movies they let their children watch to whether they bottle or nurse, or use cloth or disposable diapers. Parent-shaming is often mom-shaming, bound up in ongoing conflict and stereotypes about how we see the role of the mother."

It is possible to acknowledge legitimate concerns about sharenting without shaming parents. One common issue is that parents post photos of their children without considering how their child feels about what is being shared, or how they might feel in the future. "We're going to look back on our internet activity like bad tattoos," comments Thomas, "wishing we hadn't posted things and not being able to erase them." A 2019 study by Microsoft showed that 42% of teens have a problem with their parents posting about them on social media. They may find photos of themselves embarrassing, which is no small deal when you're a teenager, and an even bigger deal when their online footprint will one day be used to judge them as potential candidates for a college, a job, or even a romantic partner.[2]

More troubling is the fact that once posted, data such as photos are difficult to erase or even keep on one platform. In 2019, *The New York Times* report-

---

NOTES

1. In 2018, the UK Children's Commissioner report "Who Knows What About Me?" estimated that parents now post an average of 1,300 photos of a child before their 13th birthday. The report pointed to research suggesting that by 2030 two-thirds of identity theft committed against young people would be as a result of information shared by their parents.
—

2. In France, which has strict data protection laws, the police have issued warnings to parents to avoid sharing photos of their children on Facebook. In 2016, French legal expert Eric Delcroix told *The Daily Telegraph* that "In a few years, children could easily take their parents to court for publishing photos of them when they were younger." The law has yet to materialize.
—

ed about a woman who uploaded photos of her children to Flickr in 2005 and then found them being used by a military surveillance database to train facial-recognition algorithms 14 years later. "We should expect that both kids and parents will continue to be surprised over time about where their data has gone," says Plunkett.

Considering the real benefits of sharenting and the deep penetration of social media into the weft of our daily lives, it is impractical to tell parents not to share any photos of their children. Rather the focus should be on sharing mindfully and making considered decisions about each post. "Every family is going to need to do this calculus on their own," says Stacey Steinberg, a law professor and author of *Growing Up Shared*, "just like they decide when they're ready to leave their teenager at home alone, or let their third-grader cross the street without holding hands. These are all calculated choices we make as parents. We do the best we can based on the information we have, and we hope we make the right choice."

"We'll look back on our internet activity like bad tattoos."

For Peter Lok, who with his wife, Amber, shares photos of their young children to over 300,000 followers on the Instagram page @leialauren, it's a question of thinking carefully about the children's future. "We are very selective of what we share," he says, "and if there ever comes a day where they do not want to be in the public eye, we are always able to delete the account. The decision lies in their hands." He is also open to transferring ownership of the account when the girls come of age. "Social media will be the way of their world," he says, "and when they are ready, they will take over."

If Lok ends up passing the account over to his daughters, he will be enacting a new digital version of an age-old rite of passage—the moment a parent lets their child grow up and acknowledges their agency to define themselves. Yet this is potentially a handover that the children will want before their parents are ready. Adolescence is a period of experimentation, and kids today try out versions of themselves online just as previous generations did when selecting the rock bands they listened to or the fashion labels they wore. If a parent posts about their child from a young age, or even makes and runs a separate social media account for them, are they robbing the child of their right to curate their own online presence, or even to decide whether they want to be on the internet at all?

Thomas gives the example of one of her son's friends, who wanted to transition gender as a teen, but struggled to express this online because their parents had already created a social media profile for them using the gender they were assigned at birth. Thomas argues parents should not use children as "a prop for their storytelling," or seek to define them before they have had a chance to define themselves. "My son today is a lot of who I assumed him to be when he was little," she says, "but he is also someone who I never could have imagined."

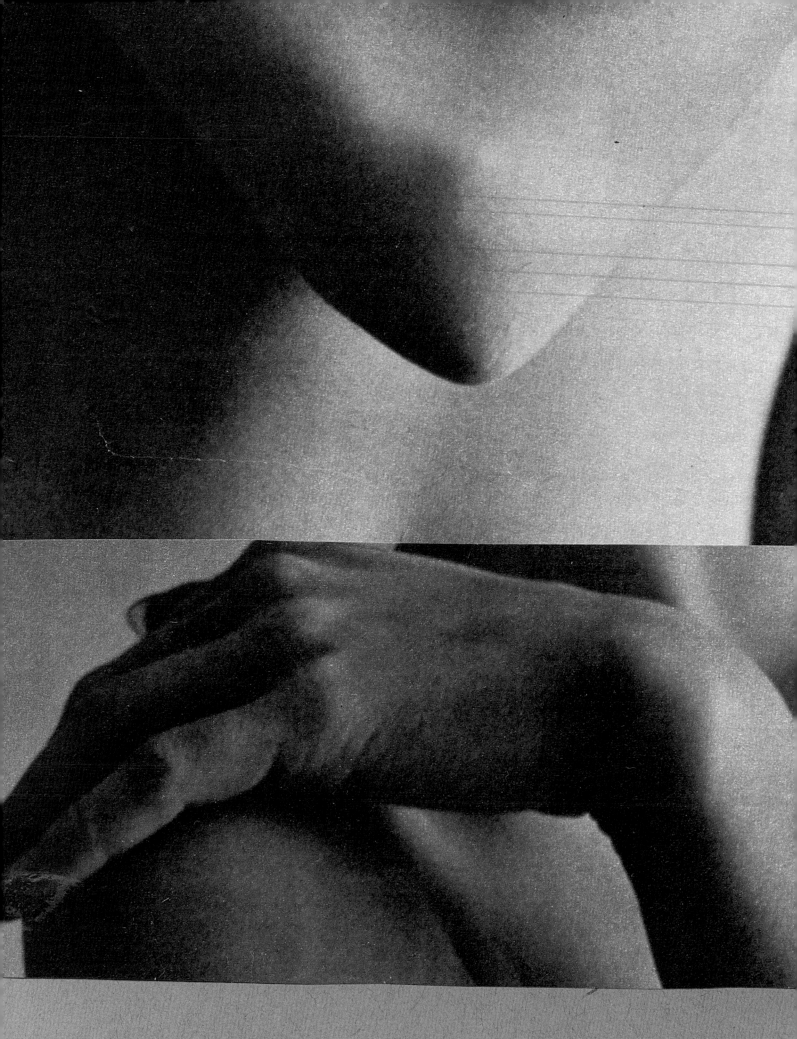

All Artworks by *Katrien De Blauwer*

FIVE TIPS:

I   LEARN

LENIENCE   II

PAY IT

FORWARD   III

BE ACCOUNT
—ABLE   IV

THINK BACK

V   GROW UP

Learn Lenience

It is hard to overestimate the impact of the car on American life at the beginning of the 20th century. John Steinbeck once wrote, perhaps hyperbolically, that "Most of the babies of the period were conceived in Model T Fords and not a few were born in them."

There is always something that is credited with marking a shifting point from one generation to the next. Vehicles. Music. Technology. And generally speaking, whatever it is tends to rankle the generation that came before. Boomers thought Gen Xers were lazy and cynical. Gen Xers thought millennials were entitled brats. Millennials think Gen Zers are TikTok slacktivists. Gen Z will surely find something to complain about in 20 years' time.

And this is not a trend specific to the modern era. In around 470 B.C., Socrates wrote: "The children now love luxury; they have bad manners, contempt for authority; they show disrespect for elders and love chatter in place of exercise." Four hundred years later, Aristotle wrote of young people that "they think they know everything, and are quite sure about it." In 1771, a letter in *Town and Country Magazine* complained that "a race of effeminate, self-admiring, emaciated fribbles can never have descended in a direct line from the heroes of Poitiers and Agincourt."

So it seems that once they've moved past the first blush of youth, people are doomed to experience a collective amnesia that erases the fact that being young is difficult. You're figuring out how to play the hand you've been dealt, moving into a world that doesn't take you seriously—that thinks you're self-absorbed, entitled, soft-bellied. If every generation levying the same criticisms against the young for 2,000 years tells us anything, it's that each generation isn't really so different from the last.

Maybe then, it's time to break the habit. Instead of putting up walls between generations, we can model something more like a peaceful transition of power which recognizes the things that make us similar. Young people may be listening to different music than we did, but they still gravitate toward music that's transgressive, and defies the norm. They may be using technology that baffles at first, but they're using it to find their voice and to speak their minds in exactly the same way we used to. The causes they fight for might be different than ones we fought for, but they're still fighting. And one day, they'll be middle-aged and cranky, too.

Pay it Forward

At crucial junctures in life, many people have been guided toward the light by the hand of an experienced advisor. A well-chosen mentor can bring direction to young people lost in an increasingly fraught job market. For the mentors, meanwhile, working with young people can be a way to not only give back, but to learn new things. Canadian academic Roxanne Reeves, who has both studied mentorship and frequently mentored others, shares her tips on supporting a young person.

SP: *What life experience or professional qualities do you think a mentor should draw on? And what should a mentee bring to the relationship?* **RR:** I think foundationally you should examine your philosophy or ideas around moral virtue and ethical behavior. If you're mentoring youth, it's really important to focus on serving with the best interest of the mentee. And to know how to be an outstanding mentee is to understand how to be an excellent lifelong learner.

SP: *What's the best way to start a working relationship with a mentee and establish a healthy dynamic?* **RR:** A trusting environment and a level of security needs to be in place. Both parties need to understand what their obligations and expectations are for the partnership.

SP: *What part does diversity play in the dynamic between mentors and mentees? Some mentees may be marginalized and interested in a mentor with a similar identity.* **RR:** It's really important to tee up mentors and mentees, but mentors are usually introduced to the concept of implicit bias in the training. Once they hit a certain level of competency, and a certain level of comfort in the role, however, they should consider branching out beyond what's a natural fit. Individuals over time will need a constellation of mentorship relationships.

SP: *Is it better to be mentored by someone a few years ahead of you, or someone with decades of experience?* **RR:** It falls into the same concept of having a variety of mentors. Some will be drive-by—they're going to give you some great wisdom, give you some remarkable direction and off they go. Other mentors will be a season, and then others will be lifelong.

SP: *The job market is wildly different from what it was 10 to 20 years ago. How can older mentors effectively apply their experience to the needs of young people today?* **RR:** I would suggest mentors recognize there are many roles in mentorship. I encourage those who want to give their mentees a career leg up to increase their role as a champion to the mentee by providing sponsorship. By sponsorship, I mean that they call somebody else on behalf of the mentee. Sponsorship means being an active champion.

Be Accountable

In the summer of 2020, Maddie Ziegler—best known for appearing in Sia's "Chandelier" video when she was 11—posted an earnest apology to her Twitter feed. Videos of her laughingly engaging in "ignorant and racially insensitive" behavior when she was nine were circulating online, and the internet demanded an explanation.

"I'm honestly ashamed and I'm truly sorry for my actions. The decisions I made then are absolutely not the decisions I would make today," the then-17-year-old wrote. "We have all made mistakes in our lives and as we grow up we educate ourselves and learn to be better people."

In her contrition, the *Dance Moms* alum joined in a new tradition of celebrities apologizing for the online misbehavior of their childhood selves. In recent years, we've seen Justin Bieber, at 20, apologizing for a "childish and inexcusable" racist joke caught on camera when he was 15; beauty vlogger Zoella, at 27, apologizing for offensive Twitter posts from eight years earlier; and Camila Cabello, at age 22, apologizing for racist Tumblr posts from when she was 14 and 15.

On some level, you have to feel for them, growing up young and dumb without the mercy of privacy. It's one of those areas where, for once, stars really are just like us—or at least like the Gen Zers and younger millennials who spent their formative years online, unknowingly setting their own traps.

Offensive language is offensive no matter the age of the speaker, but there's something farcical in Ziegler soberly asserting she's not the person she was at nine—a child apologizing for childishness. Her apology, along with the outrage that prompted it, raises an interesting question: What's the age of responsibility for online transgressions?

When it comes to criminal justice, there's an underlying assumption that youth doesn't disqualify you from culpability. In Scotland, the age of criminal responsibility was only recently raised from eight to 12, while in Qatar, kids as young as seven can be convicted of crimes. In America, where most states have no minimum age for responsibility, more than 30,000 kids under the age of 10 were arrested between 2013 and 2018.

But youth justice advocates have long maintained children should be afforded more leniency and empathy for their actions, particularly because the effects of putting them through the system (which disproportionately targets the poor, people of color and other vulnerable communities) can last a lifetime. Also, studies have shown the prefrontal cortex—the brain's decision-making center—doesn't fully develop until 25 and, in the West, young people tend to age out of delinquency by their early 20s.

Instead, groups like the National Juvenile Justice Network suggest that young offenders be diverted to restorative justice programs that emphasize taking responsibility for one's actions and making amends with affected victims and communities. While you may be too young to go through the criminal justice system, they posit, you're never too young to be held accountable.

Learning to take responsibility is an essential part of growing up, no matter who you are, and how we respond when we're confronted with our past misdeeds (including our digital ghosts) is a show of character. So apologizing, while uncomfortable and embarrassing, is never a bad thing, not really. What matters most is how we proceed going forward.

This is the position in which Ziegler and co. now find themselves. Without the threat of punishment (none of the celebrities mentioned have been incarcerated, or canceled) they've been given the opportunity to acknowledge their wrongdoings, express regret and put it on record that they've matured past the ignorance of youth. Now, they have the rest of their adult lives to prove it.

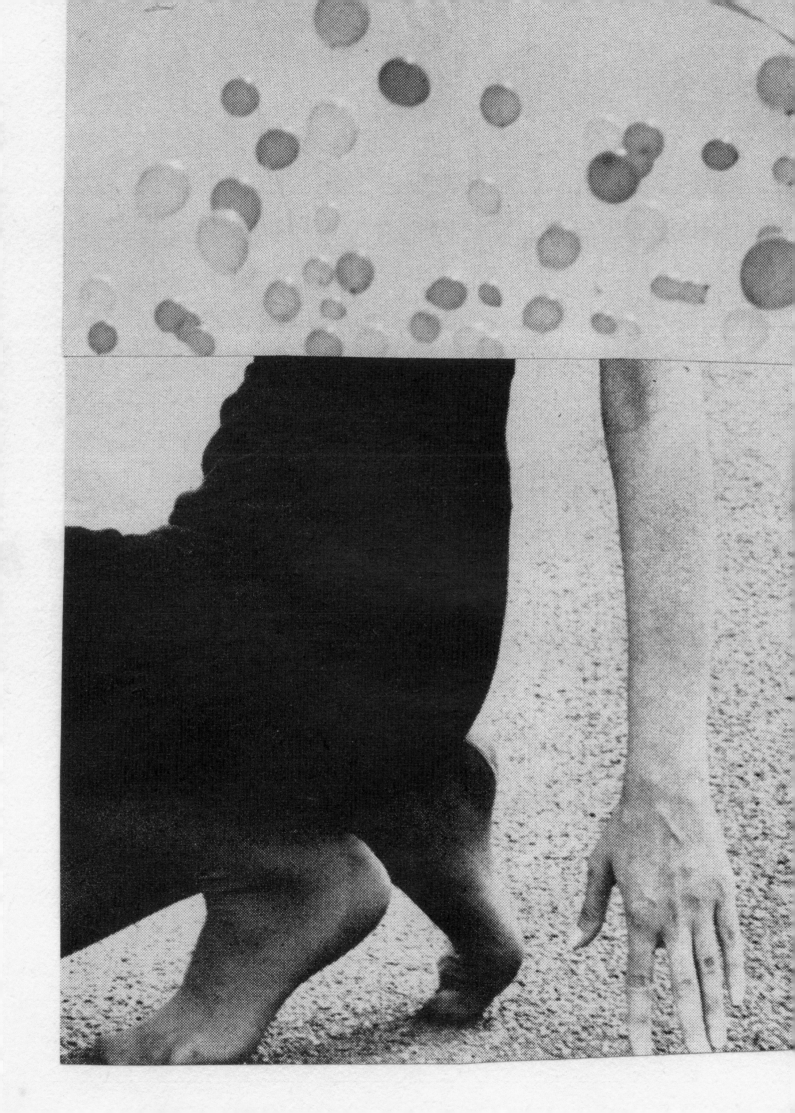

Think Back

Youth may be wasted on the young but that doesn't mean the young are impervious to the siren call of nostalgia. That's what the Canadian cultural critic David Berry argues in his 2020 book *On Nostalgia*, which sifts through a wide array of history, art and pop culture to examine just what nostalgia really means, and why it affects 20-year-olds and 80-year-olds just the same. Over Zoom, Berry explains the dual nature of nostalgia and why today, with the influence of the internet, it feels more all-pervasive than ever before.

RS: *What first sparked your interest in nostalgia?* **DB:** Basically, I was seeing it everywhere, but in what I felt like were two very weird ways. I'm a critic for the most part, and I would run across it either as the subject of a work of art, where it was always a very deep and meaningful thing. And then, on the flip side, there was this really weird contempt, a real resistance to it, especially in the form of the "Hollywood is doing another remake" kind of thing, or a band doing a reunion tour.

RS: *You write that, "One of the bitterer truths that nostalgia helps us deal with is the fact that we so rarely know when things are ending." How do you think nostalgia functions as a coping mechanism?* **DB:** I think it helps us to realize that things are, in fact, over. The sort of dual nature of nostalgia—the really wanting to go back and then the kind of slow, trickling realization that we will never be able to—forces us to confront that a lot of things about our life are already over, and were over before we could give them any sense of closure or sense of finality. Or even just process the fact that they were ending. And I think that's one of the great tragedies of life.

RS: *Do you think that nostalgia is intrinsically tied to aging?* **DB:** I think that's the core of it. The two top times in which we seem most nostalgic—or supposedly are— is either in the late teens and early 20s, just past high school, or when we're seniors. The latter makes a lot of sense: You're toward the end of life, so naturally you're looking back at all the things you did. But the first one struck me as really weird.

But if you think about it, it's an era of transition, right? You need to figure out who you are. So, in a way, I think it seems very natural that you would be drawn back to however much experience you have. In the case of a 20-year-old, it's not that much, but it's the core, it's all you really have to base yourself on. The instant time travel exists, I think that nostalgia probably ceases, for the most part.

RS: *Do you think we're growing more or less nostalgic as a society?* **DB:** We're not evolving to become any more nostalgic. But I think the opportunities for it—and the ability to indulge in it, which is key— have never been as prevalent. I have a phone in my pocket where I can access every piece of artwork that has ever been recorded, but also, my own personal history. It used to be a really big deal when you found a bunch of love letters in an attic. Now, they're indexed, and I can just search them.

Grow Up

Canadian psychologist Elliott Jaques coined the phrase "midlife crisis" 55 years ago, which means the term itself is poised for a wobble of its own. It's certainly the case that midlife crises today are more a subject of ridicule than serious psychological enquiry—they are an all-singing, all-dancing popular culture trope.

As in films such as *Sideways*, *Lost in Translation* and *American Beauty*, when we visualize a midlife crisis, we see a middle-aged man confronting his swiftly vanishing youth, the looming inevitability of death and his perceived lack of achievements by making drastic changes to his life. He often responds by attempting to change the course of past decisions and striving to reclaim his youth—perhaps by quitting a serious job to pursue a dream, buying a flashy car and fashionable clothing or leaving a long-term relationship for a younger partner.

Less a response to change than to continuity, midlife crises tend to be associated with men—perhaps because they have historically had more control over their life trajectory than women. But for any gender, it's easy to see why middle age might generate psychological upheaval: After all, our society's worship of the young and the push to unrelentingly pursue arbitrary goals set us all up for a crash when we confront life's disappointing realities.

Personal crises of any kind are multifaceted and varied, and their solutions complex and specific. But at some stage, we all experience that feeling that our youth is disappearing and we would rather it did not. The question is: Can you reclaim your younger years gracefully? Can you hold down a responsible job while clubbing every day until 4 a.m.? Can you fit a new, high-adrenalin hobby around your personal commitments?

These answers, of course, depend on you. But in deciding whether to plunge down that tunnel, it's worth considering that middle age itself is a cultural construct. Since Jaques introduced his theory in 1965, global life expectancy has risen from 55 to 72. In Western Europe (where the idea of midlife crises was born) it is now higher than 80—and in many of these countries, it is older people who hold the bulk of the power, financial clout and personal agency. Maybe, then, upon reaching middle age, we should be looking forward, not backward—looking at the years and opportunities that stretch ahead, and not the ones that we've left behind. Then, when confronted by crisis we might feel less of an urge to cling on to the superficial trappings of youth, and more of a desire to seek out and embrace the comfort, security and self-assurance that many find only in their later years.

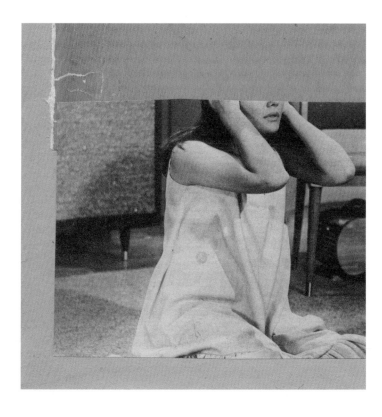

In praise of aging. Words by *Debika Ray*

4.

Directory

178—192

Peer Review

The Book of Trespass author *Nick Hayes*, on how environmentalist *Roger Deakin* taught him to engage with the natural world.

I first came to Roger Deakin's work through the words of his friend and collaborator Rob Macfarlane. In Macfarlane's 2007 book *The Wild Places*, he travels around the British Isles in search of the essence of "wild": what it means, where it is, how we humans connect with it. Inevitably, he ends up at Deakin's door. It was his description of Deakin's Suffolk home—the 16th-century farmhouse he had renovated from a rotten, disused shell purchased in 1969—that instantly turned its owner into something of a legend for me.

Macfarlane's words made Walnut Tree Farm seem alive—its oak beams creaking like a boat in a storm, the bindweed crawling through the plumbing, the foxes that had made a den in the fireplace. The house seemed to be an extension of the writer and environmental filmmaker himself, in a constant process of permeating and being permeated by nature. To me, Deakin was like a real-life version of Rooster Byron—Jez Butterworth's protagonist in the play *Jerusalem*—someone who lives on the edges of what is deemed acceptable society in order to be closer to what he considers meaningful.

It turned out that Deakin wrote books too. Those books, *Waterlog*, *Wildwood* and his posthumous *Notes from Walnut Tree Farm*, taught me that all I needed to venture beyond the world of electric lighting was a sleeping bag and a sense of curiosity. They pushed me out into the magnificent nights and cold mornings of sleeping rough in nature's cradle. Deakin had died by the time I read his words, but I made a pilgrimage to his house and, at the kindness of its present owners, was able to spend an afternoon walking through the real objects of his descriptions: the moat he swam in every book, the woods he planted, the trees he grafted together in homage to David Nash's *Ash Dome*. There was a distance between the normality of what I saw before me, and the wonder of their descriptions in his book. I wasn't disappointed. Instead, I learned something about how I could relate to the world around me, use my eyes and ears in harmony with my imagination and wonder, sidestep science and empiricism, and engage with the world in a more phenomenological manner.

WATERLOG
by Nick Hayes

Roger Deakin's first book, *Waterlog*, is a swimmer's journey around Britain. It takes a "frog's-eye view" of the world, exploring the streams, rivers, lakes and dykes that cut through Britain by immersing the reader, with the writer, into them. In one sense, it is simply a description of one man's fascination with water, but in another sense, it is a manifesto for wild freedom, the pull of nature that is not so much for the scenery, or the health, but as a way of connecting to a wilder, more animal side of us, one that can act, or swim, for the very pleasure of being alive.

A prophetic history of the almanac.

KATIE CALAUTTI

Object Matters

For as long as humans have looked to the sky and soil to predict upcoming events, almanacs have existed to help them. The word "almanac" itself dates so far back that no one can agree on its origin—guesses range from a Spanish Arabic derivation to a play on the Ancient Greek word for "calendar."

With its roots in astronomy, early iterations of the almanac were calendars that charted moon phases and the rising and setting times of the sun. The Ancient Greeks and Egyptians included festival dates in their almanacs, while Romans pinpointed lucky and unlucky days to do business and Medieval versions added holy days.

Once the first printed version was distributed in Europe in 1457, their popularity became widespread. Starting in the 1600s, almanacs emphasized scientific developments and researched data over unfounded prophecies, and they eventually evolved throughout Europe and America to include weather predictions, tide tables, proverbs, jokes, short stories, and health and gardening advice. By the 1700s, almanacs were as popular as the Bible—everyone from farmers to fishermen to domestic workers relied on their compelling mixture of scientific and folkloric alchemy.

Benjamin Franklin authored one of colonial America's bestselling publications, *Poor Richard's Almanack*, from 1732 to 1758; his singular wordplay and witticisms helped sell upwards of 10,000 copies a year. And in 1792, the *Old Farmer's Almanac* was founded—it remains America's oldest continuously published periodical. In his days as a lawyer, Abraham Lincoln famously used an 1857 copy of the publication to win a murder trial by debunking witness testimony with the almanac's lunar chart. Long before the National Weather Service was established, the *Old Farmer's Almanac* utilized a top-secret mathematical formula to create its long-range weather forecasts, which farmers still routinely plant and harvest by. To this day, it claims an 80% accuracy rate and distributes about three million copies a year.

To maintain relevance, modern publications like the UK's *Whitaker's Almanack* and the US *Almanac of American Politics* have broadened their scope to cover subjects including government, education, history, geography and transportation. Almanac archives live on as detailed time capsules of social and environmental trends, and though technology has mastered many of their elements, the almanac's appeal is rooted in wisdom ancient enough to outlive even the smartest phone or GPS satellite.

STEPHANIE D'ARC TAYLOR

Cult Rooms

In mid-century Long Island, Mary Callery's unremarkable barn sparked Mies van der Rohe's architectural imagination.

New York's Long Island, a short drive from Manhattan, is an unlikely trove of modernist architecture. Audacious homes by mid-century luminaries like Richard Neutra and Frank Lloyd Wright pepper the island. But the modernist gem with one of the flashiest backstories may be the one with the least remarkable exterior: a barn.

The story begins in 1930, when New York socialite Mary Callery left her old life—including her husband and young daughter—and sailed to Paris to open a sculpture atelier. The daughter of a wealthy couple, she probably wasn't living as rough as many of her fellow expatriate artists and writers had done in the preceding decade. But the fact that she came from money didn't preclude her from captivating the Paris avant-garde.

This cosmopolitan cohort, members of the so-called Lost Generation, quickly adopted the sculptor and model into their milieu. Callery later rapturously described these heady Paris days, "when life looked beautiful, quivering with dreams of the mind." Man Ray photographed and sketched her; Alexander Calder gifted her a brooch with her initials. In 1938, Pablo Picasso sketched a striking portrait of her head, oblique from behind, with à la mode rolled curls at the nape of her shapely neck.

Callery's friendship with Picasso would open doors for her when she fled Paris as the Nazis took over in 1940. When she arrived back in New York, she was in possession of more Picasso works than anyone else in the United States.

Her salad days in Paris, her moveable feast, were over by then —although she would continue to return to Paris for short visits. But her time there informed the rest of her life, personally and professionally. Her primary artistic preoccupation remained sculpture. But given the nature of her work—hard materials like bronze and steel swirling and softly interwoven—it's little surprise she felt a personal and professional affinity with architects. Her best-known work was commissioned by Wallace Harrison, the architect responsible for New York's Lincoln Center and the Metropolitan Opera House. To this day, it hangs on the proscenium arch of the opera. Even if you've never seen it, it's possible to deduce that the piece is abstract given its affectionate nickname: "Spaghetti Spoon in Congress with Plumbers Strap."

Shortly after returning to New York, Callery embarked on a romantic affair with the German-American architect Ludwig Mies van der Rohe. Mies, as he's known, had been the last direc-

Photograph: Gordon Parks/The LIFE Picture Collection via Getty Images

tor of the Bauhaus, the seminal school of modern architecture forced to close by the Nazi party in 1933. Among the fruits of their relationship was the barn he renovated in Huntington, on Long Island's North Shore.

From the outside, the barn is wholly unexceptional—it looks exactly as quotidian as its name implies. This was by design. Mies was struck by the original bones of the barn, and wanted to retain its austere integrity. He did, however, pick up the whole thing by its foundation and move it—to give those inside a better view of Long Island Sound.

Inside, Mies kept the structural beams in their original dark wood color, filling in the spaces in between with basic fiberboard painted white. The effect is similar to Heian-era Japanese interior architecture—white panels set off by long black lines— a famous fascination of the Bauhaus. It was a fitting neutral backdrop to Callery's ever-burgeoning art collection. She amassed it under the name Mrs. Meric Callery to imply that there was a husband in the picture, which, after her second divorce in 1936, there wasn't.

Today, Callery is better known for her collector's eye than her sculpture, and the barn is not open to the public. Like Callery herself, it's keeping its secrets.

DAPHNÉE DENIS

Bad Idea:
Feel-Good Fables

Beware the viral act of kindness.

"How do I ever say thank you?" wept 89-year-old Derlin Newey, a pizza deliveryman from Utah, as he received a $12,000 tip from a family of loyal customers who crowdfunded the sum through their TikTok channel. The video of Newey's bemused reaction after being presented with the check was shared far and wide as a welcome break from the anxiety-inducing news cycle. But in reporting the heartwarming tale of a community coming together to support one of its senior workers, most outlets failed to address the elephant in the room: Should anyone in their late 80s be working full-time in the first place, let alone during a pandemic?

An ever-growing trove of viral stories purported to restore one's "faith in humanity" follow a similar pattern: Praise is heaped on an outsized act of kindness, all the while avoiding hard questions about the societal failure that led to that person's hardship in the first place. "Donations to an 84-year-old 'essential worker' who was injured on the job are like putting wallpaper on gaping holes on the wall," says Nora Kenworthy, an associate professor at the University of Washington, Bothell, whose research on medical crowdfunding has found that 90% of campaigns do not meet their goal.

Not only does the narrative behind these "feel-good" tidbits distract us from larger issues, but by highlighting certain tragedies deserving of our attention, it creates an insidious hierarchy between the people deemed worth saving, according to Kenworthy. She says, "Rather than talking about everyone holding certain basic rights on the basis of a social contract, we're focused on helping exceptionally deserving or tragic individuals. And, of course, what's invisible here are the millions of people who don't get help but also need it."

There is certainly beauty in the fact that strangers can rally to help someone in need. Communities organizing in the face of an absent, or shredding, social safety net should be saluted. Still, framing stories of societal neglect as uplifting news items is shortsighted at best, dangerous and irresponsible at worst. Failure to question the status quo should not make us feel good—it should make us feel furious.

BELLA GLADMAN

Last Night

What did designer *Yinka Ilori* do with his evening?

London-based designer Yinka Ilori is known for throwing the full paint box at his graphically pleasing objects and spaces. At home, he's inspired by Aaliyah, food and the celebratory visual culture of his Nigerian family.

BG: *What did you do last night?* **YI:** I worked until 7 p.m. at my northwest London studio. I've been doing 12-hour days. Then I went home to do more work, listening to music. I flit between head down, making mood boards or sketching for public-realm projects, then head up, watching music videos on TV.

BG: *What music videos are you watching right now?* **YI:** I'm obsessed with old Aaliyah, Timbaland, Tweet, Missy Elliott—they remind me of my childhood in the '90s and '00s. I recently rewatched Aaliyah's first film, *Romeo Must Die* (2000). I always wonder what the music industry would be like now, if she was still here.

BG: *And what would you be doing with your evening if you weren't working?* **YI:** I'd be eating, definitely—at Pitanga, in Fulham. They serve Nigerian food with Western influences, like jollof rice fried balls and beef pepper stew. It'd ideally be a friends and family affair! When I was growing up, our house was the party house. My mum would always ask me to invite everyone round!

BG: *How has your family influenced your work?* **YI:** The celebratory feel I express through color, pattern and form has come from my relatives who are proud of their culture. In any given opportunity they'll wear clothes, whether Swiss voile lace or *aso oke*, that identify them as Nigerian. When you wear your traditional attire, you stand out! That's the beauty of color, and the work that I do. Where I live, it's boring brown and horrible gray brick: The only color is the blue sky. I like transferring the color from our clothes onto architecture—taking the fabric and wrapping a building or underpass. It's an extension of my identity.

BG: *What's your next project?* **YI:** We're finishing off one of our public commissions for 2021. I love making work for public spaces, because anyone can access it. I remember not feeling like I belonged in a gallery when I was growing up, and it doesn't need to be that way.

GOOD IDEA

by Pip Usher

The best viral campaigns seek to provide systemic solutions, not quick fixes. When Manchester United striker Marcus Rashford learned of the British government's decision to cancel food vouchers for vulnerable schoolchildren during the 2020 summer term, he wrote a heartfelt open letter that disclosed his own experiences of childhood poverty. After it was shared with nearly 13 million of his followers across Twitter and Instagram, and picked up by national newspapers, the government announced a "Covid summer food fund." In November 2020, Rashford proved that his ability to transform public sentiment into policy is enduring, when he forced a government U-turn on winter food funding also.

The sharp-eyed writer on high society and her supermodel past.

CHARLES SHAFAIEH

Susanna Moore

The early life of writer Susanna Moore reads like a fairy tale. Before she became the acclaimed author of nonfiction books and novels, including the 1995 erotic thriller In the Cut, she had modeled on The Tonight Show, read scripts for Warren Beatty and Jack Nicholson, befriended "fairy godmothers" like Alyce Kaiser (wife of industrialist Henry Kaiser) and Joan Didion and attended dinner parties in Los Angeles with Audrey Hepburn and Christopher Isherwood. But fairy tales have their dark sides too. Violence and abuse—as well as the effects of losing her mother at a young age—temper the glamour and romanticism. Moore's autobiography, Miss Aluminum, published in 2020, is a carefully constructed portrait of lost worlds and of a young woman trying to come to terms with her own identity.

CS: Clothes almost become characters themselves in Miss Aluminum, influencing how others saw you and how you saw yourself. When did you first grasp their power? SM: As a child, I learned that clothes and appearances could be both disguises as well as forms of aggression: a way to protect yourself, to put yourself forward. My grandmother would get elegant, couture clothing from the woman for whom she worked as a maid and recut them for my mother. Ironically, that's what happened when Mrs. Kaiser sent me her beautiful couture clothes that weren't particularly suited to a 17-year-old. But they were all I had. They led people to assume things that were not true. That I was rich, for example. I probably put on airs, too, in imitation of my mother and grandmother who were very intent on manners. I still stand up when someone, even someone younger and particularly a woman, comes into a room—and I'm old! Those are their ghosts haunting me.

CS: It's a kind of performance—the creation of personas. SM: As a teenager, after my mother died, I was quite wild and rebellious. It was a way of getting attention. My being outspoken and saying "fuck" all the time was also, in some ways, my absolute refusing to be female. That was a performance. Later, I was performing as a model. I was a little self-conscious and ashamed, not because I thought I was better than that, but about exposing myself in that way. If a photographer said, "Look sexy!" I would be appalled! But I have girlfriends who, the minute someone is taking their picture, still know what to do with their legs, their mouths. I look at them in awe!

CS: There were occasions where it seems you were quite self-effacing, such as at celebrity-filled dinner parties. SM: It was hard for me to pretend to be someone other than who I was, but, as I wrote, I wasn't quite clear about who I was. I was very clear about who I was not, though. I knew I wasn't a good model and definitely that I wasn't an actress. I wasn't sexually driven the way some women are, and I envied them a bit, because that was also like being a man, especially in those days. I knew I was intelligent, though, and found in books a way of being, identifying with Maggie Tulliver and Isabel Archer.

The devices I used were to be porous, to keep my mouth shut, to be amusing, and to be interested—which I was. I'm often asked questions such as, "If I was going to be sitting next to Jimmy Stewart, I would be a nervous wreck! How did you do that?" I wasn't insistent upon myself and was a good listener. And I think I was funny. My silence worked to my advantage: People told me things.

CS: You're an acute observer. But memoir writing hinges on memory, too. Was recalling these events a simple process? SM: What's interesting about memory is what you don't remember. I sent the manuscript to the people who appear in it and said that if they found anything disquieting, distasteful or inaccurate I would take it out. That's a kind of censorship, but I owed it to them. I had some facts wrong but, in one instance, so did my brother. He said the story about us going to the zoo after our mother died was lovely but didn't happen. I'm sure it did and told him he had to trust me. Then, over the next weeks, he sent notes telling me little snippets came back to him, which was very moving.

CS: Like all your work, Miss Aluminum is carefully constructed, both in content and style. For example, you don't speak about your or others' lives outside the period detailed here. How much of that was a conscious decision? SM: I could have commented throughout with the acquired wisdom and experience of the 50 years since the events, but I thought I didn't need to do that. It should be evident in the writing itself. I didn't want to be vindictive or write a tell-all, and I didn't want it to be about how I became a writer. Writing about writing is often very platitudinous. I wanted to show the part that I played in all these events without being lachrymose, self-pitying or too neurotic. That counters the glamour, beauty and famous people in the photographs. I thought the stories I tell would reveal quite a bit about me. I hope so.

A new head-scratcher
for spring.

ANNA GUNDLACH

Crossword

ACROSS

1. Canine companion?
6. Racetrack shape
10. High point
14. Get out of the way of
15. Grouter's piece
16. Asian sea that has almost completely dried up
17. Young horse who invented revolvers?
19. Wander the internet
20. Famous line in *A Streetcar Named Desire*
21. Revolutionary Trotsky
23. Disco lover on *The Simpsons*
24. Informal negative
25. Singer with a role in *Mamma Mia! Here We Go Again*
27. Garden pest
29. Understood
30. Young goose who starred in *La La Land*?
32. Come after
34. Apt (but unwelcome) rhyme for "eye"
35. End in ___ (draw)
36. Hot-spring resort
38. Bear's lair

40. The only Black man to win Wimbledon
43. ___ bro (Silicon Valley stereotype)
47. Software test versions
51. Young sheep who was a famed English essayist?
54. Nutritional stat.
55. Central body part
56. Ancient Roman garment
57. Undulating Lay's variety
58. CRT successor
59. Editorial slant
61. Rubs the wrong way
63. "Just playing with you!"
65. Young salmon who costarred in *Blackadder* and *Jeeves and Wooster*?
67. Casino numbers game
68. Not as much
69. Flavor of ouzo and absinthe
70. Razor feature
71. Sparkling wine area
72. Nervously walks back and forth

DOWN

1. Text or email
2. Enthusiastic acclaim
3. Weeps over
4. No longer young
5. Fishing spool
6. Not needing an Rx
7. Like many M-rated video games
8. Cause of sneezing and wheezing
9. Jared of *My So-Called Life*
10. Common batteries
11. Do something extremely well, in slang
12. Cocktail with vermouth
13. Keebler cookie brand
18. Frilly
22. "Panini" rapper Lil ___ X
26. Comes down with
28. Geometric surface
30. Gym unit
31. Reference with over 20,000 pages, for short
33. App operators
37. Grabbed a bite
39. Flow back
40. Masquerade as
41. Like someone whose monocle just fell out

42. *I, Tonya* subject
44. Gigantic properties
45. Most accessible
46. Wizened old woman of fairy tales
48. Cause of a commuter's delay
49. Causing harm, like a side effect
50. Assents to
52. Easy toss
53. Speed of sound measurement
57. "You game?"
60. Land in el mar
62. Disorganized pile
64. Mother deer
66. Abbr. on the side of a tire

ANNICK WEBER

Correction

Teenagers aren't lazy, they're exhausted.

"Life moves pretty fast. If you don't stop to look around once in a while, you could miss it." Such are the wise words that teenage anti-hero Ferris Bueller uses to justify skipping school for a little fun with his friends in the 1986 movie *Ferris Bueller's Day Off*. His words ring true to anyone living in today's fast-paced times, but they're especially pertinent for adolescents. More than other age groups, teens really do need an occasional break from life's hectic obligations.

It has long been believed that teenagers are lazy—that they're constantly finding ways to slack off in order to lie around doing nothing. Medical research, however, suggests that it's time retire this myth. Upon hitting puberty, the human brain changes, and with that, there's a shift in the circadian rhythms that govern the body's clock. While most children and adults function best when they go to sleep and get up early, teens are biologically conditioned to stay awake later and sleep in: Their brains don't secrete the sleep-inducing hormone melatonin until about 11 p.m. and it stays in their system until at least 8 a.m. So in an adult-designed world, where school starts early, teenagers suffer from chronic jet lag.

As a result of inadequate sleep, adolescents often lack the energy they need to focus in the classroom. They aren't actually unmotivated slugs; they're just tired. A number of studies have proven that teens perform better (and are less likely to consume energy-boosting drugs, alcohol or cigarettes) when they can get up later for school, while keeping their usual bedtime. Rather than calling teens lazy, isn't it time to adapt school schedules to their natural rhythm? After all, as Ferris Bueller once pointed out, we might otherwise deprive them of living their lives to the fullest.

Several teenage clichés may be partly attributed to circadian misalignment: sleep deprivation has been shown to lead to memory issues, mood swings and trouble concentrating.

Stockists

ACNE STUDIOS
acnestudios.com

ADIDAS
adidas.com

AMERICAN VINTAGE
americanvintage-store.com

AMI PARIS
amiparis.com

ANDREW COIMBRA
andrewcoimbra.com

BALENCIAGA
balenciaga.com

BLUEMARBLE
bluemarbleparis.com

BOSS
hugoboss.com

BOTTEGA VENETA
bottegaveneta.com

BOUTET
boutet-official.com

CARHARTT WIP
carhartt-wip.com

CHANEL
chanel.com

CONVERSE
converse.com

COS
cosstores.com

DANSKO
dansko.com

DIOR
dior.com

FALKE
falke.com

HELMUT LANG
helmutlang.com

HERMÈS
hermes.com

HOUSE OF FINN JUHL
finnjuhl.com

HYEIN SEO
hyeinseo.com

ISSEY MIYAKE
isseymiyake.com

JW ANDERSON
jwanderson.com

KANGHYUK
kanghyuk.net

KENZO
kenzo.com

LANVIN
lanvin.com

LATRE
latreartandstyle.com

LESET
leset.com

MAISON KITSUNÉ
maisonkitsune.com

MARKOO
markoostudios.com

MARNI
marni.com

MARSET
marset.com

MAXELL
maxell-usa.com

MIU MIU
miumiu.com

MOTHER
motherdenim.com

MOTOROLA
motorola.com

MUTINA
mutina.it

NINTENDO
nintendo.com

NOGUCHI BIJOUX
noguchi-bijoux.com

NOUVEAU RICHE
shopnouveauriche.com

OLYMPUS
cameras.olympus.com

PERRY ELLIS
perryellis.com

PH5
ph5.com

PICCOLO SEEDS
piccoloseeds.com

POLLY WALES
pollywales.com

POST ARCHIVE FACTION
postarchivefaction.com

PRADA
prada.com

ROUJE
rouje.com

SALOMON
salomon.com

SALVATORE FERRAGAMO
ferragamo.com

SIMONS
simons.com

SONY
sony.com

STRING
stringfurniture.com

TAMAGOTCHI
tamagotchi.com

TANT D'AVENIR
tantdavenir.com

UNIQLO
uniqlo.com

VANESSA DE JAEGHER
de-jaegher.com

VANS
vans.com

WHITE BIRD
whitebirdjewellery.com

YOWE
yowe.kr

Note to Self
154 — 161

ABBY STEIN

Dear pre-teen Abby/YA:
I know, you feel alone. You
are a girl the world isn't
listening to. They claim you
are a boy. You should know:
· You are not alone - there
are millions like you!!
· You CAN do it. You
will survive, and a fun,
successful life is waiting
for you.

Live on. Rock on.
With love,
Abby C Stein, 2020
PS: Pay more attention to
mommy's cooking...

MICHAEL BARGO

Dear Michael,
Always be true to yourself
and trust your instincts.
Your dreams will come true,
just don't give up!
Hang in there!!!
xo MO

MICHAËL BORREMANS

Hey Michael,
You here out of the future.
(took some trouble to get
here...) Important: I did
not let you down regarding
dreams and aspirations!
Cheers to that!!! Wish we
could hang out together,
would be fun and hilarious
with this age difference!
But hey, in a way we do!
Miss you! Yours, You.

ANDRÉ ACIMAN

Dear André,
I remember so well
the day you turned
seventeen. I remember
your insecurities, your
dreams, your loves, your
resentments and regrets,
your thirst for so many
things, some undefined,
others still unknown,
maybe unreal. I remember
them because I've never
outgrown them—and hope
I never do. I know you're
coddling many hopes,
and I know you've taught
yourself not to trust them,
because you've known
failure and fear it no less
than you fear success. Here
is my advice: learn to trust
what's in your heart now,
even if it seems a whim,
and don't let it die or be
dulled away by what we call
wisdom and experience.
Don't waste your time,
as I did, pursuing what
others taught me to seek.
Seek instead what, despite
risks and challenges,
thrills you and makes you
happy. Don't fight it. You
may adapt but you won't
change. Stay who you are!
Yours,
The older you, André

AI-DA

And touch the soil again. A

RODERICK COX

Dear Roderick,
A couple of tips to help you
along the way...
1. Depth to your work
comes from Experience
and hard work.
2. There is no substitute or
shortcuts to preparation.
3. You ~~will~~ must become
your most important
teacher
4. A Healthy self-confidence
must be...
· nurtured
· protected
· evaluated
5. Examine what you don't
know and fill in the gaps.
6. Reflect! Then move on.
7. As a musician, always
sing! Never hold back!
Leave everything on stage!
8. Don't tear someone down
to build yourself up.
9. Always be grateful.
10. Opportunities may not
always come when you
expect them to, but be ready
when they do!

All the best to you!
Roderick

Credits

COVER
Photographer
Ted Belton
Stylist
Nadia Pizzimenti
Hair
Ronnie Tremblay
Casting
Marc Ranger
Models
Whak and *Mo* at Next
Canada

Whak wears a shirt, jacket
and trousers by Homme
Plissé Issey Miyake, scarves
by Simons and shoes by
Converse. *Mo* wears a
shirt by COS, a jacket and
trousers by Homme Plissé
Issey Miyake, socks by
Simons and shoes by Vans.

NEW CHALLENGE
Art Director
Zalya Shokarova
Hair & Makeup
Sasha Stroganova
Models
Olya, Nastia, Vlad, Andrey

SHELF LIFE
Parisian architect *Joseph
Dirand*'s living room,
featuring a painting by
Lawrence Carroll, a console
table by *Joseph Dirand*
and objects by *Georges
Jouve, Adrien Dirand,
André Borderie* and *Robert
Rauschenberg.*

THE AFTERGLOW
Producers
Kelly Bo & Cho Hyunsoo
Photo Assistant
Donghwan Lee
Fashion Assistant
Bokyeong Go

Features designs from
Central Saint Martins
graduate collections:
Soyoung Park,
@soyoung.p_; *Hyejin Kim,*
@otakurace_.s2;
Keewon Shin, @lxeewon.

BREATHING ROOM
Photo Assistant:
Esteban Wautier

AWKWARD
Hair & Makeup Assistant
Ian Russell

SPECIAL THANKS
*Ekaterina Bazhenova-Yamasaki
Kelly Bo
Kira King
Mishka
Vinatería, New York*

My Favorite Thing

Interior designer *Pierre Yovanovitch*, interviewed on page 46, tells the story behind his favorite piece of furniture.

My home is filled with all of my favorite things, but if I had to choose one, it would be an oak-wood chair that I designed 10 years ago. It was the first object I created for the house. Since it's made of only one material—natural wood—it feels solid and strong. It has the proportions of a sculpture more than it does a piece of furniture. At first glance, it looks like it might be uncomfortable to sit in, but in fact it's the opposite: You can sink right into it, like a favorite armchair. I have two of these chairs at my house.

I'm not planning on making more, as I want them to remain unique. They're usually in the kitchen—the room where I spend the most time. I love to cook and eat, and I often have friends over so the chairs are always at the center of everything. They are quite heavy, but sometimes I move them into the living room, where I like to sit by the fireplace. All my furniture is intended to be used, nothing I do is purely decorative. It would go against my beliefs if design didn't have a purpose.